Nearly a decade ago, a Canadian mutual fund company with an eye on international markets retained an investment counselling firm known for its international expertise. It was a good fit. The entrepreneurial flair of BEA Associates proved the perfect complement to the ambitions of the company which eventually became known as C.I. Mutual Funds.

Fast forward to the present. Both companies have undergone extraordinary changes to meet the challenges of an increasingly complex and competitive marketplace. What has not changed, however, is the recognition that in the knowledge-based investment industry, success depends on finding and working with the top money managers.

Bill Sterling and Stephen Waite are among the best in their field. In an era of information overload, they are masters at producing profitable and practical applications for investors. BOOMERNOMICS is a perfect example of exhaustive research into demographics, with all its financial, social and cultural implications, being applied to the development of pragmatic and effective investment strategies.

We hope you find this book both an interesting and insightful look at a subject which will inevitably influence the course of our lives in the coming years.

MUTUAL FUNDS

BOOMERNOMICS

The Future of Your Money in the
Upcoming Generational Warfare

WILLIAM STERLING
STEPHEN WAITE

THE LIBRARY OF CONTEMPORARY THOUGHT
THE BALLANTINE PUBLISHING GROUP • NEW YORK

The Library of Contemporary Thought
Published by The Ballantine Publishing Group

http://www.randomhouse.com/BB/

Mr. Sterling and Mr. Waite are employees of BEA Associates,
a member of Credit Suisse Asset Management. The views they express in
this book, however, are their own and may or may not be the views of BEA
Associates. Additionally, Mr. Sterling and Mr. Waite may or may not factor
certain of these views into their activities for BEA, but are under no obligation
to do so. In expressing their views herein, Mr. Sterling and Mr. Waite are
not intending to provide advice or issuing reports or analysis regarding the
purchase or sale of specific securities. Finally, no statements in this book
should be construed as an offer to sell or a solicitation to
purchase any securities.

LIBRARY OF CONGRESS CATALOGING-IN-PUBLICATION DATA
Sterling, William Paul.
Boomernomics : the future of your money in the upcoming generational
warfare / William Sterling, Stephen Waite.
p.   cm.
ISBN 0-345-42583-9 (hc: alk. paper) ISBN 0-345-43293-2 (pbk: alk. paper)
1. Economic forecasting—United States.   2. United States—Economic
conditions—1981–   3. Investments—United States.   4. Baby boom
generation—United States.   I. Waite, Stephen R.   II. Title.
HC106.82.S74   1998
338.973'001'12—dc21   98-26814
                                                             CIP

Text design by Holly Johnson
Cover design and illustration by Ruth Ross

Manufactured in the United States of America

First Canadian Edition: September 1998

10   9   8   7   6   5   4   3   2   1

To our families

Contents

Preface

These are the good old days.
—*CARLY SIMON*

IN THE HILLS of ancient Egypt, one of the earliest economic forecasters had to interpret a dream about fat calves and withering crops. With that, a young man named Joseph made a great call about a long run of prosperous years followed by a long run of lean years.

Fast-forward four thousand years to the end of the twentieth century. We have just experienced what are conceivably the greatest five years in all of humanity's history. The world is free of large-scale military conflict. We are in the midst of the most remarkable upsurge of knowledge and wealth ever seen on this planet. Dazzling technologies whirl around us. Information flows at the speed of light. New drugs and medical technologies promise to make our lives longer and healthier.

Focusing on the American economy, we find that these are truly extraordinary times. America is at the vanguard of the information and life sciences revolutions. Blessed with its technological lead, its sophisticated financial markets, and its currently unchallenged geopolitical dominance, America is well positioned to be the major beneficiary of the trend toward global economic integration.

Economic anxiety, in vogue just a few years ago, has given way to unbridled optimism (some would say irrational exuberance). America has restored its position as the world's fiercest competitor. Business has boomed and consumer confidence has soared to levels not seen for several decades. Real wages have begun to rise after a long period of stagnation. In an economy that has created nearly seventy million new jobs over the last fifteen years, employment opportunities abound for those willing to work. Inflation, the nemesis of the 1970s and 1980s, has been vanquished. The red ink associated with years of massive federal budget deficits has turned to black. Investors have enjoyed a breathtaking rise in stock prices, which have more than doubled in the past five years. Long-term interest rates have plunged to levels not seen since the 1960s.

As the gap between rich and poor widens, the fruits of America's economic progress remain unevenly shared. But for most Americans it appears as if the good old days are right now. The big question is whether the good times will continue.

Our answer is yes. To be sure, the business cycle remains a fact of life and we should continue to experience market volatility and normal economic fluctuations. There may even be an abnormal business cycle disturbance in the year 2000 if what's being called "the year 2000 computer glitch" turns out to be as serious as some analysts contend. But considering all the favorable trends that are now in place, the next decade should represent another golden era for the American economy. With the baby boom generation entering its prime earning years, we call this upcoming decade America's Prime Time.

Unlike Joseph, our call is based not on dreams but on the future that has already happened. Our vision is called "boomernomics" because it's mainly about how seventy-six million American baby boomers are transforming the economy. But it's also about how the boomers themselves are being transformed by a stunning technology revolution that we believe is still in its infancy.

America's Prime Time should continue to be a great time for investors. As millions of baby boomers enter their peak years for both earning and saving, we expect interest rates eventually to fall to shockingly low levels while inflation remains largely absent from the scene. This would set the stage for stocks to continue to set one new record after another, making the wildest bulls end up seeming timid. Every indication is that the high-tech revolution should bring a cornucopia of new goods, services, and jobs. Despite the recent turmoil in Asia, capitalism should continue to go global while America remains in the driver's seat of the world economy.

The lean years will come, but not until later, when the boomers begin to retire in large numbers. This retirement wave starts in about 2010 and doesn't stop for twenty years. One of the goals of this book is to show you what could happen and help you deal with it. First, housing prices will slump badly as the boomers downsize their homes and move to warmer locations. Then the U.S. stock market enters a prolonged, agonizing bear market as elderly boomers liquidate their holdings to fund their retirement needs. The tech revolution reveals its darker side as incredible advances in artificial intelligence displace ever-larger numbers of workers, including white-collar and professional types. The gap between the haves and have-nots widens to a chasm.

Generational warfare erupts as the baby boomers' children and grandchildren revolt against punitive tax increases needed to care for the elderly boomers. Inflation makes an insidious comeback as government deficits and debt explode under the weight of tens of millions of baby-boomer retirees who live mainly on Social Security and Medicare. America's standing in the world economy erodes steadily as newly confident emerging nations catch up with our technology and military prowess. Considering the slump in the U.S. stock market, young investment strategists overseas dismiss the United States—along with other Group of Seven nations—as poorly run nursing homes in terminal decline. We call this period the Big Chill.

The scenario we paint may sound like something out of a Hollywood horror film script, but to our own horror, much of it is based on a huge body of mainstream economic research that is woefully underappreciated by Wall Street money managers, Washington policy makers, and the general public. It is also based on the commonsense observation that demography is destiny. If anything about the future is predictable, it is simply this: The boomers will get older.

Even if you doubt that our political leaders will meet the challenges of the age wave, we believe that a boomernomic perspective will help you in managing your own financial affairs. A successful investor must have some view of the future. Understanding the age wave should give you an edge in understanding likely prospects for your home's future value, the major trends in financial markets, and your children's career prospects. Boomernomic thinking should also help you anticipate what sectors of the economy are likely to experience booms and busts. That information should give you the key to prospering in the good times and surviving the bad.

Acknowledgments

This book is the product of a chance conversation between our friend John Alderman of Merrill Lynch and our editor Peter Gethers of Random House. We are grateful to John for his salesmanship about some of our previous research reports and to Peter for his enthusiasm and careful guidance throughout the research and writing process. The book also has its origins in some work we did in 1995 and 1996 on demographics and financial markets that was prompted by discussions with our client Bill Holland of C.I. Mutual Funds and with BEA Associates' CEO, Bill Priest. Thanks to both Bills for stimulating our thinking and for encouraging our research. We would also like to thank two friends in Washington, Pete Davis and Tom Gallagher, for some helpful conversations and research references. We have also benefited from numerous conversations on demographics and financial markets with our colleagues at BEA Associates, including Ian

Borsook, Bob Justich, Bob Moore, and John Praveen. Thanks also to Ian Borsook, Alice Sterling, Cora Sterling, Michael Sterling, George Sterling, and Lisa Waite for reading the manuscript and providing detailed and constructive comments. Naturally, none of those named above should be held responsible for any errors we have made, nor should it be assumed that they agree with our conclusions or scenarios. Finally, thanks to our wives, Cora and Lisa, and our children, Erin, Michael, Allison, and Madeleine, for their love and support throughout the project.

Introduction

The Predictable Baby Boomers

G IVEN THE RECORD of many modern economic and financial forecasters, readers may question whether there has been much progress made in the field of forecasting. Ask your stockbroker sometime why his or her firm's economic and financial forecasts for inflation or interest rates have decimal points. If he or she is honest, the reply is likely to be: "To show we have a sense of humor." That said, as a species we humans have distinguished ourselves by our ability to look ahead and plan accordingly.

Demographics—the study of human populations—is invaluable to investors. One of America's most well known bond investors, Bill Gross, put it this way: If he had to go off to a South Seas island without any source of communication for the next few years, the one thing he'd want to know when it came to structuring his investment portfolio would be demographics.

Baby boomers like to think of themselves as highly individualistic and unpredictable. In reality, as a group, much of their economic behavior has been highly predictable. Depending on what stage of life the boomers are in, they have had massive effects on numerous industries and the overall financial markets. This should continue as the boomers pass through their middle years and into old age.

THE PIG AND THE PYTHON

Demographers have used the image of a pig slowly passing through the body of a python to describe the massive displacement created by the baby boomers as they have passed through different stages of life. The image captures an important fact: The boomer generation is huge compared to both the preceding generation and the following generation. That has had enormous implications for every market that the boomers have touched. Whenever the boomers reach a new stage of life, demand for related products soars. The result is a long boom. When the boomers move on and no longer buy a product, demand slumps. The result is a bust. For any products or services that are related to the stage of life the boomers are passing through, paying close attention to the movement of the pig in the python is critical.

The first boom, not surprisingly, was in baby products. After the GIs came home from World War II, they and their sweethearts immediately and enthusiastically started making babies in record numbers. One of the first firms to feel the impact of the boom was Gerber, which saw its sales double between 1948 and 1950. Strong sales of baby food continued

FIGURE 1. BABY BOOM, BUST, AND ECHO

Number of Live Births in the United States

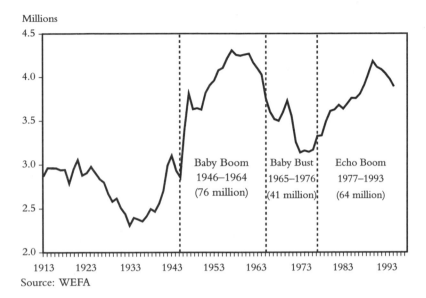

Baby Boom
1946–1964
(76 million)

Baby Bust
1965–1976
(41 million)

Echo Boom
1977–1993
(64 million)

Source: WEFA

until well into the 1960s. Then came the birth control pill in the mid-1960s. The birth rate slipped, and baby food sales quickly plummeted. Gerber was then forced to diversify into other businesses such as life insurance and child care.

That simple pattern of boom and bust has been repeated in one industry after another throughout the postwar period. For example, America's school system was swamped in the 1950s as boomers stormed the kindergartens and elementary schools in large numbers. A boom in elementary school construction quickly ensued. Not coincidentally, the boom was associated with a shortage of well-qualified schoolteachers. In 1957, the nation worked itself into a panic about the quality of education after the Russians launched the Sputnik satellite. That hysteria highlighted how the needs of the boomers were beginning to become central to the nation's agenda.

Should it have been surprising that the sexual revolution occurred in the 1960s, when tens of millions of teenage boomers were surging with hormones? Was it a coincidence that the nation focused on "family values" or "parenting" in the 1980s, when massive numbers of thirtysomething boomers were raising their own children (the so-called echo boomers)? Should it have been surprising that a huge boom in real estate occurred in the 1970s and 1980s? That's when tens of millions of boomers competed against one another to acquire homes, pushing prices into the stratosphere.

Likewise, the double-digit interest rates of the 1970s were at least partly related to the huge surge in demand for mortgages and consumer loans coming from the young boomers. Like most twenty-year-olds, the boomers were basically broke in the 1970s. Naturally, they needed to borrow money in large amounts to buy their first cars, their first homes, and the furniture to fill those homes. Competing against each other, they drove the price of money sky high as they piled on massive amounts of debt.

BOOMER VERSUS BOOMER

A corollary of what happens in markets when the boomers enter on the demand side—that is, prices go up—is what happens when they all try to sell something at the same time: obviously, prices of whatever they sell en masse tend to get pushed down. The labor market has been an important case in point.

As a huge crowd of boomers shed their bell-bottoms and entered the labor market in the 1970s, it quickly became a buyers' market for entry-level workers and remained so for several decades. Competing against each other for jobs, the boomers not only depressed wages for several decades, they also contributed to the nation's productivity slump by reducing the incentive for firms to make substantial capital investments. Why invest in laborsaving machinery when labor is plentiful and cheap? The data are striking: From 1970 to 1989, real per capita income grew at an anemic 2.2 percent per year. That compared to robust growth of 4.0 percent in the 1960s.

Just as the boomers had crowded each other in schools, they crowded each other in the labor markets, depressing each other's wages in the process. As we discuss later, the same dynamic is likely to affect the real estate and stock and bond markets after the boomers retire. They will then reach a stage of life when they will be natural sellers of stocks, bonds, and real estate to finance their twilight years. That is likely to depress prices of their hard-earned assets.

We've talked about the boomer generation as if it is one monolith. But it is important to understand how different the life experiences of the older boomers have been from those of their younger siblings or relatives. The front-end boomers are those born in the late 1940s and early 1950s. The back-end boomers are those born in the late 1950s or early 1960s. To be sure, all boomers experienced some of the same inconveniences—crowded schools and crowded labor markets. From a demographic perspective, however, the front-end boomers had it much better than their younger siblings or relatives.

Consider the housing market. The front-end boomers started to buy their first homes in the early to mid-1970s. That left them well positioned, along with their parents, to enjoy a rocket-ship ride in the real estate market as their homes soared in value when the younger boomers came into the market in force. In contrast, back-end boomers paid astronomical prices for their first homes, thanks to the huge demand created by their elders. The back-enders also encountered depressed labor markets just as they entered their prime home-buying years.

Naturally, once the older boomers were established with their leading position in the real estate game, they were able to trade up to higher-priced homes as their careers advanced. That left them well positioned to benefit from the surge in demand created by younger boomers who followed them into the trade-up game.

DILBERT DYNAMICS

Many front-end boomers also enjoyed a big advantage in the labor market for a simple reason: Corporations are organized as pyramids, with many entry-level jobs at the bottom and few choice management jobs at the top. As front-end boomers entered the job market, they found a relatively small cohort of Depression and war babies ahead of them in corporate structures. Ambitious front-end boomers therefore had a relatively easy time moving up through the ranks of companies in the 1970s and 1980s, occupying the choice positions ahead of their younger siblings. As Canadian demographic experts David Foot and Daniel Stoffman note, the baby boom forms a huge rectangle when viewed on a graph of the population distribution. The problem is that it is very difficult to promote a rectangle up through a triangle. At the top of the corporate pyramids, space is limited.

Life is like a movie theater. The people who show up first invariably get the best seats. In this sense, the demographic dice have been loaded heavily against the boomers born in the late 1950s or early 1960s. They arrived late to the crowded job market, finding the best positions already taken by their elders. They also arrived late to the real estate market and had to pay exorbitant prices for homes. Adding insult to injury, back-end boomers bought their homes just in time for a softening of real estate markets in the early 1990s. That real estate slump was related to the dearth of demand caused by the baby bust.

Back-end boomers have also arrived late to the stock market party and retirement savings game. Once again, they are at a disadvantage because of the year of their birth. Back-end boomers who wish to build retirement nest eggs are now forced to pay much higher prices for stocks and bonds compared to the prices paid by their elders. They can also expect much lower returns.

Nothing symbolizes the overcrowded and highly competitive job market better than the ubiquitous work cubicles that are lampooned in Scott Adams's *Dilbert* comic strip. The real-life cubicles were built to cheaply accommodate huge numbers of new entrants to the labor force. Dilbert's world of overworked and underpaid lackeys reporting to imbecile bosses (front-end boomers?) reflects the unfavorable demographics that have plagued baby boomers in the labor market.

PREDICTABLE BOOMERS IN AN
UNPREDICTABLE WORLD

Our focus in this book is not on the boomers' past but on their future. Many aspects of that future are highly predictable: For example, boomers will need record numbers of hearing aids and will put a great strain on the nation's Social Security system. We are not so naïve as to believe that we can forecast the future with pinpoint accuracy. Predicting the future is difficult, and we confidently predict that it will always be so.

The Pig-and-the-Python metaphor is apt with respect to demographic forces, but the problem is that the python itself is being buffeted by external forces that can be random and chaotic. Does this mean that it is completely pointless to try to look ahead over the next several decades? We think not. Following management expert Peter Drucker, we believe that the best way to approach the future is to identify major events that have already happened, irrevocably, and that will have predictable effects over the next several decades. In other words, we believe that it is fruitful—and profitable—to identify and plan for the future *that has already happened.*

Barring war, pestilence, or being hit by a comet, demographics is the most important and obvious force that has clear and predictable implications for the next several decades. Therefore, boomernomics—the economics of the baby boom generation—will focus largely on demographic trends.

THE WILD CARDS: TECHNOLOGY AND GLOBALIZATION

Beyond demographics, there are two other major, fundamental, and irreversible economic forces that will shape the next decades. The first is the technology revolution, which is clearly in progress with great force. The second is the trend toward global economic integration, something that has also been under way for several decades.

If demographics represents the predictable element in our economic future, the twin forces of technology and globalization represent the chaotic and unpredictable. As technology pundit George Gilder notes, "Anyone who predicts the technological future is sure to soon seem foolish. It springs from human creativity and thus consists of surprise."

The same could easily be said about the future course of globalization, which is supported by the information revolution but is also crucially dependent on politics. Who could have predicted the speed of the collapse of Communism? Who knows how long America's political system will continue to support free-trade policies that promote higher long-term living standards at the expense of short-term job losses?

Our assumption is that no one will be able to turn back the clock on either the progress of technology or globalization. If anything, both forces look set to accelerate rather than recede. As a result, our focus will be on the basic character of these forces—that is, on how they are likely to affect the lives of the boomers—rather than trying to forecast what particular technologies will succeed in the marketplace and when.

One thing is perfectly clear: The "clock speed" of the

global economy is accelerating. In almost every field, minor and major innovations are appearing more rapidly than in the past, thanks to better communications and increased competition. The global pool of research talent continues to grow rapidly, with China alone producing three hundred thousand new engineers per year. Moreover, a huge drop in international telecommunications costs and dramatic growth in the Internet are increasing the speed and frequency of research communications needed to produce technology breakthroughs.

The near certainty of further massive declines in international telecommunications costs—what Frances Cairncross of *The Economist* calls "the death of distance"—is key to our view that global economic integration will continue to accelerate in coming decades. Even if politicians try to resist the trend toward globalization, we believe they will be frustrated by what former Citicorp chairman Walter Wriston has called "the twilight of sovereignty." Nations pursuing economic policies that do not make sense increasingly run the risk of having their financial markets and national currencies quickly crushed by an ever-wakeful network of global investors and traders.

Financial markets are demanding increasing transparency and accountability from countries that wish to be part of global capital markets. That now includes almost every nation on the planet. This trend puts political leaders in the same position as corporate managers who are subject to a round-the-clock voting process on the wisdom of their strategies. The voters are the well-informed and highly motivated investors, traders, and analysts who dominate global financial markets.

From our perspective of trying to look ahead, we are less interested in the exact path that globalization will take and more interested in how the basic trend will affect baby boomers' career and investment opportunities. Today's reality is that software programmers in San Jose or Toronto are in direct competition with programmers in Bangalore, India. If we are correct, such competition will spread through most white-collar professions. That will simultaneously erode job security for some workers even as it creates big opportunities for others.

THE PLAN OF THIS BOOK

Obviously, any number of future scenarios can be drawn from different combinations of the demographic, technological, and global trends we have discussed. To sharpen our focus, we consider just two major scenarios that are shaped primarily by demographics—the most predictable force of all. The first, our America's Prime Time vision, is about the next dozen or so years when the baby boomers are passing through their peak years of earning and saving. As noted in the preface, this scenario looks remarkably benign, with the potential to be wildly bullish. Part I contains an overview of key demographic trends as well as our thoughts on technology and globalization.

Part II, in which we discuss our Big Chill scenario, is about the two decades beginning around the year 2010, when the baby boomers begin mass retirement. As noted in the preface, it is quite predictable that, barring a miraculous productivity dividend from the technology revolution, the nation will face daunting economic challenges in this period. Other rich, developed nations such as Canada, France, Germany, Italy, and Japan appear to face even more daunting demographic challenges, so the problems in these years are likely to be global in scope. In describing the Big Chill scenario, we will pay particular attention to likely trends in real estate and financial markets and the inevitable strains on Social Security and Medicare.

That America faces a profound transition as it demographically becomes "a nation of Floridas" is, in our opinion, virtually certain. How traumatic it turns out to be will depend on whether baby boomers, as individuals, plan wisely for their retirement years and—critically—properly influence the economic policies put in place over the next decade. In Part III we pick up on the theme of Pablo Cruise's hit song, "Whatcha Gonna Do?", and consider a variety of strategies that baby boomers and their political leaders can use to prosper during the coming demographic transition. If we all—individually and collectively—understand the challenges ahead, the good news is that we should be able to take advantage of the favorable environment of the next decade to prepare for the boomers' retirement years.

Part I

AMERICA'S PRIME TIME

Let the good times roll.
—*THE CARS*

THE GREEK PHILOSOPHER Aristotle was one of the first disciplined students of the aging process. Working on the subject between 340 and 335 B.C., he viewed young people as hot-tempered and fickle, lacking in self-control, preoccupied with honor and victory, and naïvely optimistic. Lacking a sense of political correctness, he described the elderly in largely unflattering terms: cynical, small-minded, contemptuous of others' opinions, and slaves to the love of gain.

Ever fond of the Aristotelian mean, he was far more flattering about men in their prime:

> They have neither that excess of confidence which amounts to rashness, nor too much timidity, but the

right amount of each. They neither trust everybody nor distrust everybody, but judge people correctly. Their lives will be guided not by the sole consideration either of what is noble or of what is useful, but by both; neither by parsimony nor by prodigality, but by what is fit and proper. . . . They will be brave as well as temperate, and temperate as well as brave.

Aristotle concludes that "the body is in its prime from thirty to thirty-five; the mind about forty-nine." We conclude that Aristotle must have been middle-aged when he wrote all this!

Let's assume that Aristotle was right about our peak years. If we were living in a preindustrial society, where brawn was more important than brains, the fact that many citizens have passed their physical prime would be a big economic problem. Fortunately, we live in a predominantly service-based economy, where brains and discipline matter the most for economic productivity.

In the modern era, workers tend to reach their peak productivity in their forties and fifties, before slowing down markedly in their sixties. With the boomer generation moving into its peak years of earning, saving, and perhaps even wisdom, the nation's demographic profile looks quite favorable, at least for the next decade. The economy is on a roll, and there are plenty of reasons to expect the good times to continue over the next decade.

Let's look forward to America's Prime Time.

1

Baby Boomer Demographics: It Doesn't Get Any Better Than This

WHAT ECONOMIC TRENDS should we look for during America's Prime Time? In our view, the trends are already clear: robust growth and productivity, low inflation, low interest rates, and generally buoyant financial markets. If anything, the surprise could be how long these conditions last, how far interest rates end up falling, and how high stock prices rise during this period.

These trends not only are due to favorable demographics, but also reflect the forces of technology and globalization that we will discuss soon. But demographics are an important part of the story in at least three ways.

First, aging baby boomers are likely to remain relatively conservative politically, suggesting steady and perhaps boring economic policy. Financial markets tend to like boring economic policy.

Second, the boomers are entering a stage of life when

they tend to be settled in their careers and are, on average, more productive than when they were trying to find themselves in their twenties or early thirties. Even those who are not wild about the self they eventually found are at least more likely to show up for work every day!

Third, boomers are at a stage of life when many people get serious about saving for retirement. As they age, they will compete with each other for a good return on their savings, which is apt to drive interest rates down and stock prices up.

As we've said, we emphatically do not believe that economic fluctuations are a thing of the past. We also expect that financial markets will experience normal patterns of volatility. There could easily be a number of violent interruptions of the bull market on Wall Street if inflation makes a temporary comeback or if economic shocks come from overseas. But the underlying trend, which has permitted corporate profits to *double* roughly every ten years, should be relatively easy to maintain during the boomers' prime years. And the prices boomers are willing to pay for a piece of those profits, which is what the stock market is all about, could easily escalate further from already lofty levels as more boomers get into the savings game. As we explain later, our optimistic scenario anticipates a Dow Jones Industrial Average above 25,000 by 2010. We also explain why we would not rule out a Japanese-style mania that pushes the Dow index above 35,000 by then.

BOOMER POLITICS: OLDER, MORE CONSERVATIVE

As the boomers advance into the next decade, we expect government economic policies to continue to foster low inflation, low interest rates, and reasonably buoyant financial markets. While there is no guarantee that policies will be particularly wise in addressing the daunting long-term challenges America faces when the boomers retire, there are good reasons to suggest that government policies will be relatively cautious about keeping spending in check and, most likely, generating modest budget surpluses.

Consider two important facts. First, people tend to become more conservative as they age. Second, the middle-aged and elderly tend to be far more conscientious about voting than the young. In 1990, for example, more than 70 percent of voters older than forty-five voted in the congressional election compared to less than 40 percent of voters between the ages of eighteen and twenty-four. Therefore, an aging society is likely to become a more conservative society, with its older members having a disproportionate voice in the political process. The tendency of people to resist new ideas as they age may have its own risks, as we shall discuss later when we consider the Big Chill scenario. For now, the conservatism of middle age appears to be a benign force for the economy and financial markets.

Middle-aged and elderly people clearly have more of a stake than the young do in voting for politicians who are committed to low inflation and low government spending. Obviously, elderly citizens who are living on fixed incomes can be devastated by inflation. Accordingly, they are likely to be suspicious of any adventuresome economic policies that would risk igniting inflation. The same can be said of aging baby boomers who are just now beginning to think about their retirement plans. Like the elderly, aging boomers will be loath to see the government inflate away the value of their hard-earned savings.

As gray hairs continue to sprout on baby boomers' heads, both major parties are likely to feel ongoing pressure to keep government spending and inflation under control. Should they be tempted to waver, they are likely to be quickly guided back to the straight and narrow path of fiscal prudence by the "bond market vigilantes." These are the professional fund managers who manage America's pension funds and mutual funds. This group is programmed to sell bonds and stocks at the first whiff of inflation or reckless government spending, and their careers are on the line if they do not protect their clients.

Commenting in 1994 on the economic consequences of America's mutual fund boom, economist David Hale drew the clear connection to American politics:

> Today, retirement plans are continuing to expand their ownership of the stock market but they are not producing a passive form of pension fund socialism. The U.S. is instead embarking upon an unprecedented experiment in the democratization of bond and equity ownership through a mix of mutual funds, defined contribution pension plans, and direct ownership of securities. American politicians have not yet fully

grasped the significance of this development because the financial markets have been in a steady bull market since the end of the Gulf War three years ago. But by the time of the next presidential election, the performance of the bond and stock markets could become more important political variables than at any other time in American history. If stock prices are rising over twenty million households will feel better about the economy, but if they are falling there could be more widespread pessimism about the economic outlook than was the case when mutual fund ownership was limited to a few million people.

It was probably in response to this type of analysis that Clinton adviser James Carville mockingly wished to come back in his next life as the bond market, "so he could intimidate everyone." In recent years, both President Clinton and his political adversaries on the Republican side have shown extraordinary sensitivity to the concerns of the bond and stock markets. This is almost certainly not because they have all become avid viewers of Louis Rukeyser's *Wall Street Week*. Instead, it reflects their rising sensitivity to gray power and the financial concerns of the aging electorate.

What is perhaps most remarkable about the current political climate in America is the reasonably narrow range of disagreement about key economic policies, at least among the major political leaders whose views matter most. In recent years, for example, there has been no real argument between the major political parties about whether to move toward a balanced budget, only about how to do so. There has also been broad bipartisan support for stable monetary policy, since neither party would like to be accused of bringing back anything like the inflation of the 1970s.

The most contentious policy issues have focused on international trade, including the decision to encourage greater economic integration with Canada and Mexico via the North American Free Trade Agreement (NAFTA), which was approved in 1993. Notably, NAFTA was approved with substantial bipartisan support under a Democratic administration. The Clinton administration has been widely accused by Republicans of "stealing Republican ideas" in many economic areas, further illustrating the relatively narrow range of policy disagreements.

Political analysts warn of growing polarization at both the far left and far right of the political spectrum, and we will return to that theme when we discuss the Big Chill scenario. But with respect to the centrism that dominates American economic policy currently, many foreign observers are most impressed by how committed both parties are to free-market principles and prudent monetary and fiscal policy. To foreign eyes, economic policy debates in America appear largely to be Tweedledum-Tweedledee discussions with little ideological content.

Maybe it's just a coincidence, but America's inflation rate in the postwar period has tended to rise and fall along with the age wave. As shown in Figure 2, the inflation rate was low in the 1950s and 1960s, when younger workers were a small fraction of the workforce. When the number of young people in the workforce, and of voting age, exploded in the 1970s, inflation also accelerated sharply. When the fraction of younger

FIGURE 2. THE AGE WAVE AND INFLATION

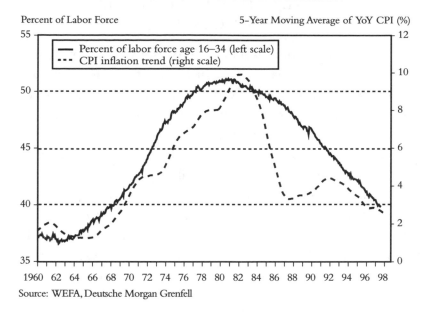

Percent of Labor Force · 5-Year Moving Average of YoY CPI (%)

Legend:
— Percent of labor force age 16–34 (left scale)
- - - CPI inflation trend (right scale)

Source: WEFA, Deutsche Morgan Grenfell

workers declined in the 1980s and 1990s, inflation settled down again.

We suspect this relationship partly reflects how the age wave affects the conservatism of economic policy. If aging boomers continue to support low-inflation policies, as we expect, then inflation over the next decade should resemble that of the Eisenhower years, when inflation averaged under 2 percent. Low inflation, in turn, would permit interest rates to remain low and would support high stock and bond prices.

OLDER, NOT OLD: THE GOOD NEWS ON PRODUCTIVITY

In modern economies, wages tend to rise with age, peaking for workers in their late forties or early fifties. Most economists believe that this pattern reflects higher productivity among older workers, even though many workers clearly begin to slow down in their fifties.

In some occupations, such as professional football, productivity and earnings naturally peak much earlier. But the vast majority of workers are not involved in professional sports, heavy manual labor, or theoretical physics. In most occupations, peak productivity arrives much later in life, and shows little decline for workers in their fifties. With older Americans getting healthier and most work becoming less physically demanding, there is little reason for pessimism about American productivity over the next decade based on demographics.

Certainly, workers in their fifties experience small declines in short-term memorization abilities and general mental quickness. But these declines appear to be more than offset by other factors, including superior judgment and organizational skills. Older workers also appear to be more likely to stay with companies longer than younger workers, thus providing a better return to companies on investments in training. A study by the American Association of Retired Persons (AARP) found that employees in their twenties tend to stay with a firm an average of 3.4 years, while those in their fifties and sixties tend to stay 15 years.

Other plus marks on the side of older workers include

fewer on-the-job accidents, less job-related stress, and far lower levels of illegal drug use. Anecdotal reports of businesses that have experimented with hiring older workers appear positive. For example, Naugles, a West Coast food chain, reported that its turnover rate dropped from 400 percent per year to 80 percent after its hiring policies were changed to focus on older workers. In short, the basic message from studies covering thousands of workers is that, aside from a slight decline in productivity in jobs requiring substantial physical effort, older workers perform as well as or better than younger workers.

If older workers are more productive and better-paid, they are also more vulnerable to a sharp cut in wages when they lose their jobs. To the extent that their productivity is based on firm-specific skills acquired over many years, older workers have more to lose than younger workers during corporate restructurings and workforce reductions. Accordingly, as the population ages, more workers may shy away from aggressive demands for better wages and working conditions, which would make them targets in a downsizing. Union organizers may debate whether growing numbers of vulnerable middle-aged employees will create a new demand for unionization. We suspect, however, that forces such as technology and globalization that have undercut union power will continue to have the upper hand.

The effect of the baby bust is another reason for optimism about productivity trends over the next decade. Other things equal, a relative scarcity of entry-level workers creates incentives for firms to invest more heavily in laborsaving equipment. But other things are not equal. Thanks to the technology revolution, the price of capital goods has been plummeting relative to labor costs. So firms in the 1990s have had huge incentives to invest in plant and equipment, and have been doing so aggressively.

The basic idea is simple: If labor is expensive and the costs of computers and other technology are plummeting, any rational business will invest heavily in technology. The data are compelling. Over the last decade, for example, employment costs have risen by 45 percent. In contrast, the price of capital goods as reflected in the nation's national income statistics has remained unchanged and the price of goods categorized as information technology has fallen an astonishing 40 percent. Not surprisingly, real business investment as a share of total economic activity rose to a postwar record of 16 percent in 1997. This trend augurs extremely well for future productivity growth.

BABY BOOMER SAVINGS: THE DOG THAT HASN'T BARKED (YET)

As the boomers move into their peak years of earning and productivity, it is logical to expect a boom in household savings. While most young people struggle to make ends meet and typically pile on debt to buy their first homes and first cars, middle-aged people tend to be wealthier. This is based partly on their accumulated savings and partly on inheritances from their parents, which usually come in middle age.

At the depth of a long bear market in stocks in 1982, University of Chicago economist Robert Aliber made a contrarian—and correct—case for investing in stocks. He supported his argument partly by describing the "personal life cycle" of investors in commonsense terms:

> Many middle-class Americans will, by the time they're in their late forties or early fifties, suddenly and unexpectedly find themselves in a position of financial ease. The mortgage has been reduced, the children are through or nearly through college, the microwave oven and the video recorder are working, and there are no more lumpy expenditures to make. All of a sudden, a new problem arises—what do with the extra money.

Aliber's view must have been music to the ears of then-struggling stockbrokers, financial planners, and mutual fund managers. With hindsight, his analysis turned out to be highly prophetic for America's mutual fund industry, which has seen explosive growth in new money to manage over the past decade. Since 1990, the industry's assets have risen nearly fivefold, from $1.1 trillion to $5 trillion. This has led many to warn against excessive speculation or "irrational exuberance," to use Federal Reserve Board chairman Alan Greenspan's phrase.

From this data, many assume that we are in the midst of a huge surge in savings by the boomer generation. Likewise, they conclude that the boomers' saving mania has been responsible for pushing up stock prices. We must confess to having shared this impression, since we have been in the front lines of the mutual fund industry, watching the money roll in.

There is one problem with this story: It's not true. There

is no doubt that mutual funds have been taking in a lot of money. And there is some evidence that at least some Americans are trying to save more. For example, a poll by the American Savings Education Council showed 69 percent of U.S. workers saving in 1997 versus 61 percent in 1964. Also, led by baby boomers, nearly 50 percent of all U.S. workers contribute an average of 5 percent of their gross income to 401(k) plans.

Here's the catch. Even if some baby boomers have been trying to build up nest eggs for retirement, many more have been piling on debt and spending like there's no tomorrow. That is reflected in the nation's most widely followed measure of household savings, which showed that the U.S. personal savings rate in 1997 fell to only 3.8 percent—its lowest level in fifty-eight years. Like Sherlock Holmes's dog that didn't bark, the most interesting aspect of the baby boomers' saving story is that the boomers do not appear to be saving in earnest.

Contrary to popular belief, it is hard to argue that American households, boomers or otherwise, have pushed stock prices up in a buying frenzy in the past few years. True, households bought an impressive $841 billion of stock mutual funds in the 1993–1997 period. But over the same five years, households sold a far greater amount—$1.1 trillion—of direct holdings of stocks. Overall, American households have been net sellers of stocks into the strong market rise of the last few years.

One factor boosting stock prices in recent years has been record share buybacks by corporations. In the 1993–1997 period, for example, corporations bought back $114 billion

FIGURE 3. WHERE ARE THE BOOMERS?

Personal Saving (% of Disposable Personal Income)

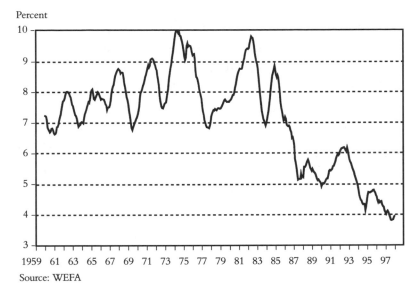

Source: WEFA

of their own shares. In effect, corporate managers have created a "shortage" of shares, which has helped boost share prices.

More important is that over the same period, reported earnings per share of the Standard & Poor's 500 companies rose by an impressive 148 percent, which is the strongest five-year run of the postwar period. Strong profit growth naturally boosts what potential shareholders are willing to pay for stocks.

The decline in inflation in recent years has also boosted the attractiveness of financial assets in general, and stocks in particular. When inflation is high and rising, interest rates also tend to rise and draw money away from stocks. When inflation is low, interest rates also tend to be low. Naturally, that prompts many investors to look to stocks for better returns.

Old-fashioned fundamentals—for example, strong earnings growth and low inflation—thus appear to be the dominant factors in the strong stock market of the last few years. If demographics have influenced stock prices, it has been indirectly, such as via the increasingly conservative political climate, which has favored lower inflation, and the higher productivity of middle-aged workers compared to young workers, which has boosted corporate profits. A surge in boomer savings does not appear to have been an important part of the story. At least not yet.

WILL BABY BOOMERS FINALLY
BEGIN TO SAVE?

There is enormous skepticism among economists about prospects for a rise in the savings rate. "Americans just don't save" seems to be the refrain.

Researchers at the Federal Reserve Bank of New York recently calculated that demographic factors are likely to push up the savings rate by less than 1 percent as baby boomers age. That projection assumes that boomers will save at roughly the same rate as their parents as they get older.

Other researchers at the Brookings Institution argue that the savings rate could actually *fall* as the baby boomers age. Older Americans apparently now save far less than previous generations. That's because America's senior citizens now count on generous government support in their retirement years, especially for high-ticket medical care. According to the Brookings research, seventy-year-olds today are consuming roughly one fifth more than thirty-year-olds; in the early 1960s they were consuming nearly a third less. Apparently all those bumper stickers that say "We're Spending Our Children's Inheritance" must mean business.

In short, there does not appear to be a strong consensus on whether the age wave will be positive or negative for overall savings. Most economists now believe the impact will be small. Accordingly, the profession has given up on the "commonsense" view that as the boomers move into their fifties, they will actually get serious about trying to save for retirement.

Certainly it's anyone's guess as to exactly when a surge in baby boomer savings will materialize. And the recent rise in stock prices may have made many baby boomers complacent that their retirement nest egg will grow rapidly without any special efforts. In our view, however, there are three reasons why the age wave will eventually drive up the savings rate.

First, the boomers need to save more than their parents did because their Social Security and Medicare benefits are likely to be far less generous than what their parents received. As we discuss later, Social Security is likely to survive in some form, but benefit levels will almost certainly be cut sharply.

Absent government subsidies and higher spending by the elderly, the Brookings research concludes that the current rate of savings in the United States would be three and a half times as large. As it becomes clear that government subsidies for retirees will become less generous, the savings rate should rise. With the debate over how to "fix" Social Security and Medicare likely to dominate politics in coming years, baby boomers will be educated *ad nauseam* on why they need to save more themselves. As we discuss later, the boomers may even be forced to save more if the government moves in the direction of a fully funded, privatized Social Security system.

Second, unlike their parents, baby boomers cannot count on their homes being good investments. Boomers are likely to be competing against each other as sellers when they retire en masse. That should put substantial downward pressure on home prices in coming years. Against that backdrop, baby boomers will have a strong incentive to pay down their mortgage debt to reduce the interest expense of home ownership. Paying down debt will require a boost in savings.

Third, boomers have no assurance that the stock market will continue to provide the high rate of return they have become accustomed to in recent years. That means that for any desired standard of retirement living, they should count on saving more rather than less. Even though we present a benign scenario for the next decade, there are a number of reasons why boomers should not assume that financial markets over the next twenty years will be as kind and gentle as they have been recently.

Ironically, a sharp correction in the stock market and/or a recession over the next few years could be positive for stocks over the next decade. Even without a recession, a sharp market pullback could prompt widespread corporate restructuring and scare more baby boomers into trying to save more. If, as a result, inflation and interest rates end up falling yet another notch, the next stock market upswing could be extremely powerful. This is especially likely if the technology revolution lives up to its promise.

2

The Technology Revolution:
We've Only Just Begun

M ANY MAY FEEL that the technology revolution has been overhyped. We maintain, in agreement with super-computer pioneer Danny Hillis, that the technology revolution is *under*hyped. If we are right, America's Prime Time should continue to be a rewarding period for investors. That's because a boom in technology investment not only should create thousands of new business opportunities and rising profits, but should also help keep inflation and interest rates low.

In our view, recent trends suggest that we are on the cusp of a productivity boom that will have far-reaching consequences for our nation's standard of living as well for future financial market performance. The potential of the Internet and other computer networking technologies to trigger major productivity gains is central to our positive view of the next decade. We also believe that we are in the early stages of what is likely to be a new epoch in the life sciences that could transform the lives of boomers and nonboomers alike in coming years.

It may be conventional to think of the United States as an industrial power, but that notion is beginning to outlive its usefulness. Today America stands at the vanguard of a revolution in information technology that is fundamentally changing the way we live, work, and play. Not only is this revolution changing the nature of commerce and how nations create wealth, it is also radically transforming how we create, store, and communicate knowledge. Looking back at the long sweep of economic history, we have not seen such an economic metamorphosis since the industrial revolution of the eighteenth century.

During the industrial revolution, the pace of economic activity and productivity growth accelerated dramatically as our ancestors learned to substitute machines and fossil-fuel energy for animal and human muscle. The underlying science of the industrial revolution was classical physics, whose basic principles were developed by Sir Isaac Newton in the seventeenth century.

During the information revolution, the clock speed of the world economy is set to accelerate further as we learn to use silicon chips, glass fiber, and biotechnology to augment, substitute for, and quite possibly surpass human intelligence. That is permitting us to gain further mastery over our physical environment and life itself. The underlying science of the information and life sciences revolutions is quantum physics, whose basic principles were developed by Erwin Schrödinger, Werner Heisenberg, and many others beginning in the first half of this century.

Interestingly, even the life sciences revolution can be

traced to quantum physicists such as Schrödinger, who dared to claim that life could be explained by a "genetic code" written on the molecules within a cell. In that sense, as physicist Michio Kaku points out, the multiple revolutions we are now experiencing can be viewed as different aspects of one revolution, namely the quantum revolution. In fact, the incomprehensibility of quantum physics itself may help explain why so many intellectuals are suffering from one form or another of what Alvin Toffler called "future shock." As renowned physicist Niels Bohr said, "Anyone who is not shocked by the quantum theory does not understand it." Put differently, if you are not just a little confused by the multiple revolutions swirling around us, you are probably not paying attention.

The boomer generation has little choice but to prepare for a faster pace of economic change, because it is privileged to live in the midst of the most remarkable upsurge of knowledge and wealth ever seen on this planet. By some measures, human knowledge is doubling every ten years, if not faster. In the past decade alone, more scientific knowledge has been created than in all of human history prior to that time. Meanwhile, growth in world wealth has been equally, if not more, impressive. Since 1980, world wealth has risen by more than 1,100 percent, from roughly $5 trillion to nearly $60 trillion in 1997.

THE AMAZING MICROPROCESSOR

As impressive as these data are, they pale in comparison with the explosive growth of computing power. Since 1950, the power of computers has advanced by a factor of roughly ten billion. At the heart of the information revolution is the microprocessor, a chip smaller than the head of a ballpoint pen and made from three of the most basic elements known to mankind: metal, sand, and air. Invented twenty-five years ago, the microprocessor is associated with the development of a host of commercial products that have become part of our daily lives. These products include the personal computer, camcorder, CD player, microwave oven, pager, cellular phone, answering machine, fax machine, and satellites, to name just a few.

The microprocessor is the driving force behind the remarkable growth in computers. Back in 1943, shortly before the first boomer cohort was born, Thomas Watson, chairman of IBM, remarked that he thought there was a world market for maybe five computers. As we know today, Mr. Watson's forecast was a bit off the mark. In 1997, global personal computer shipments totaled nearly 85 million units. Worldwide PC shipments are expected to grow at a 15 to 20 percent annual rate in coming years. At that rate, the total number of PCs shipped globally will double to almost 170 million units by 2002. Inflation-adjusted spending on information technology equipment in the United States alone was over $300 billion in 1997, up tenfold since the beginning of the decade. Spending on technology is a powerful source of economic growth in the United States today. According to the Commerce Department, the high-technology industries of computers and telecommunications accounted for more than a quarter of the American economy's growth in the last five years. The powerful surge in computer spending in recent years has defied all predictions by analysts who make their living reading the economic tea leaves.

Former business consultant and author Michael Rothschild argues persuasively that the microprocessor is the most profound technical advance since the invention of movable-type printing over five hundred years ago. Like the printing press, the microprocessor has fundamentally altered the way we solve problems. And like the printing press, the microprocessor has irreversibly changed the way we collect, store, copy, and revise knowledge. Every week, fabrication plants around the world produce over one billion microprocessors. Over the next few years, that number will jump to two billion per week. Today there is more computing power in a new car than in the Apollo spacecraft that carried our astronauts to the moon in 1969. Over the past twenty-five years, the microprocessor has had such a far-reaching effect on scientific research that it is difficult for scientists today to imagine doing research without it.

The driving force of the explosion of computing power is Moore's Law. Named after Gordon Moore, a cofounder of the Intel Corporation, the law posits a doubling of computing power every eighteen months. Moore made his now famous prediction in 1965, and over the past thirty-three years it has proven remarkably accurate. Scientists' ability to double the power of the microprocessor every eighteen months is directly related to their ability to squeeze more and more transistors on a chip. When the microprocessor was born in the early 1970s, it consisted of only a few thousand transistors. Today, Intel's Pentium II processor has over 7.5 million transistors. According to Intel's projections, by the year 2010 the microprocessor will be packed with a whopping one billion transistors.

Here is one way to put the amazing progress in microchips into perspective. First, imagine etching a map of the city of Pasadena, California, stretching from the Rose Bowl to Cal Tech, on a square the size of your fingernail. That was essentially the level of technical progress in the 1970s. Today, chip scientists are able to etch the equivalent of a map of all of North America containing street-level detail for the entire continent, on that same fingernail. At the current exponential rate of progress, the equivalent of a street-level map of the planet is not far off.

Since the birth of the microprocessor in 1971, the cost of computing has plunged ten-million-fold. Had we experienced similar cost declines and performance improvements in the commercial aircraft industry, a Boeing 767 would cost $500 and circle the globe in twenty minutes on five gallons of gas! If we extrapolate Moore's Law into the future, microprocessors are likely to be as cheap and plentiful as the paper this book is written on. As Marc Weiser of Xerox's PARC research facility has written, "Long-term, the PC and workstation will wither because computing access will be everywhere: in the walls, on wrists, and in 'scrap computers' (like scrap paper) lying around to be grabbed as needed."

Microprocessors are rapidly transforming the way we live, work, and play. One result is a tremendous increase in the penetration of new products into American households. As the economy has evolved over the past century, it has taken less and less time for new products to make their way into our lives. For example, it took fifty-five years for a quarter of American households to own a car. Likewise, it took nearly fifty years for a quarter of American homes to be wired for electricity. Installing phones in a quarter of households in

America took thirty-five years. In contrast, a quarter of American households had a PC after only sixteen years, a cellular phone after only thirteen years, and access to the Internet after only seven years.

The worldwide installed base of PCs today is estimated to be somewhere in the neighborhood of two hundred million. According to Intel, worldwide PC sales will exceed TV sales before the end of the decade. The ongoing convergence of information and communications technologies promises to significantly broaden the role of the computer in the years ahead, transforming the PC into an appliance as common as TVs or telephones. How rapidly that will occur is difficult to predict, but it seems virtually certain that the convergence of information and communications technologies will continue to transform the global economic landscape in the years ahead.

Despite the tremendous growth in the number of people going on-line during the past several years, the Internet and the World Wide Web are still in their infancy. Moore's Law tells us that microprocessors are going to become much more powerful in the future. Furthermore, all signs point to a host of innovations in communications technologies that seem likely to progress with even greater speed than Moore's Law.

COMMUNICATIONS AT
THE SPEED OF LIGHT

Developments in communications technology, spurred by developments in the field of fiber optics and innovations in satellite-based wireless services, are another likely source of radical economic change in coming years. According to some scientists, we are currently in the Stone Age of optical communications, also known as photonics. The pace of innovation in this field is breathtaking.

Telecommunications experts tell us it is only a matter of time before all homes have access to high-speed Internet service. As many people can attest, surfing the Internet today is a painfully slow process. With on-line traffic doubling every hundred days, the congestion we experience on the Net is akin to being stuck in a traffic jam on the freeway during rush hour. Fortunately, this unhappy state of affairs seems unlikely to persist for much longer, given the enormous potential of new communications technologies. Cheap, high-speed communications networks appear to be on the horizon.

While Moore's Law is driving chip power higher and higher, photonics and other innovations in communications are vastly increasing the bandwidth, or the carrying capacity, of our communications networks. Today, one strand of fiber-optic cable the width of a human hair can transmit in less than one second the content of every issue of the *Wall Street Journal* ever published. As the reach of fiber-optic network extends throughout the United States and around the planet, the power of communications networks is likely to become incomprehensible. The bandwidth of communications networks is expected to triple every year for the foreseeable future. Fiber-optic communications networks, coupled with advances in modem technology, will greatly expand the power of the Internet.

The impressive power of the Internet reflects a simple mathematical property, namely, that the value of the network rises in proportion to the square of the number of inputs. Consumers and businesses alike will benefit enormously in the future from cheaper and faster Internet connections. As costs fall, Internet usage will rise, thus rapidly expanding the power of the network.

There are varying estimates of how quickly more powerful Internet connections will arrive and the impact that such connections will have on households and businesses. According to Jupiter Communications, there will be nearly ten million American households with high-speed Internet connections by the year 2001—almost one fifth of all projected on-line households—compared with less than 2 percent today. High-speed Internet access, coupled with advances in payments and security technologies, will in all likelihood put on-line commerce into hyperdrive.

Many things consumers do routinely today, such as shopping for food, books, music, cars, and houses, paying utility bills, and purchasing airline tickets, are increasingly likely to migrate to the Internet. Businesses have already found high-speed Internet access an indispensable technology. Utilizing the latest advances in communications technologies, companies such as Dell and Cisco Systems conduct millions of dollars' worth of transactions with customers each day on the Internet.

In 1997 approximately a hundred million people logged on to the Internet. Analysts reckon that the number of Internet users will soar to a billion over the next five years. Meanwhile, the value of electronic commerce is expected to reach a staggering $223 billion over the next four years, up from just over $11 billion in 1997. According to projections by Interactive Data Corporation, electronic commerce will grow at a blistering 114 percent compound annual growth rate between now and the year 2001.

Future innovations in communications technologies will undoubtedly lead to changes that households and businesses today can't even begin to predict. Indeed, consider how mobile phones have transformed traditional communications. Because of advances in cellular communications, many of us don't think twice today about making a call from a car, train, or airplane. Rather than being a luxury item, mobile phones in the future are likely to become wearable accessories. Firms increasingly use mobile communications technology to help employees do their jobs more effectively and efficiently.

Many developing countries are now installing state-of-the-art mobile phone networks. Cellular phone penetration in middle- and low-income countries is rising at a 50 percent compound annual rate. Mobile communications networks will undoubtedly continue to play a critical role in the economic progress of the developing countries in the years ahead. These trends help explain why in 1996 mobile communications accounted for an astounding 47 percent of all new telephone subscriptions in the world. As Frances Cairncross notes in her book *The Death of Distance*, the mobile telephone may be the most successful new way of communicating that the world has ever seen.

The combination of increasingly cheap computing and low-cost telecommunications also points toward explosive growth in artificial intelligence capabilities that will boggle the mind. A map of global Internet connections already looks suspiciously like diagrams of the synaptic complexity of the human brain, and computer experts talk of the Internet as the ultimate parallel-processing machine. We have already seen the power of massive parallel processing in 1997 when IBM's Deep Blue computer soundly trounced world chess champion Gary Kasparov. Deep Blue's not-so-secret weapon was its ability to analyze two hundred million positions per second, using thirty-two microprocessors.

In a provocative book called *After Thought: The Computer Challenge to Human Intelligence*, James Bailey argues that computers will rapidly evolve a process of intelligence that is not the same as ours, or even understandable by ours. As this proceeds, Bailey predicts that "even scientists and specialists will increasingly be taking the word of electronic circuits for vital information on vital issues." According to James McAlear, "Sometime in the next thirty years, very quietly one day we will cease to be the brightest things on earth." Even if that turns out to be hype, Kasparov's defeat makes it clear that powerful computers will continue to displace humans in areas once thought to be the special province of human intelligence.

PRODUCTIVITY BOOM AHEAD?

In our view, the technology revolution will have profound implications for America's future standard of living and the performance of its financial markets. Surprisingly, many academic economists view such a claim with great skepticism, principally because there is little evidence that the hundreds of billions of dollars spent on information and communications technologies in the past decade has had any significant impact on the nation's overall rate of productivity growth. In fact, the joke among academic economists is that you see computers everywhere but in the productivity data.

How do we reconcile the fact that economists are unable to detect any significant change in the nation's ability to produce goods and services more efficiently with the myriad positive changes wrought by the information technology revolution? After all, many people know that every financial institution and many of the nation's factories would shut down if the computer software that runs their systems were removed.

Economist Michael Cox of the Federal Reserve Bank of Dallas has suggested that the usual measures of progress—output of goods and services, and productivity—lose touch in an age of rapid technological progress. He argues that as the economy evolves it delivers not just a higher level of production, but also new goods and services, improved products, greater variety, more time off, better working conditions, more enjoyable jobs, and other benefits. All of these raise our living standard but by their nature are not easily measured. Most are not even counted in gross domestic product, a commonly used yardstick of the total amount of goods and services produced in the economy.

Measurement issues aside, there are good reasons to expect a productivity dividend from spending on information and communications technologies in the years ahead. The well-known author and futurist Arthur C. Clarke once noted that people exaggerate the short-run impacts of technical change and underestimate the long-run impacts. Echoing this sentiment, Stanford professor Paul David has argued that it may take as long as forty to fifty years before new technologies' full impact on the growth of productivity shows up in conventional indicators. Professor David's view is based on analyzing the effects of networked electricity on the major industrialized countries during the first half of the 1900s.

The advent of networked electricity had a profound effect on the United States economy. It radically transformed our nation's factories, stores, and homes. To use a metaphor appropriate to the industrial age, the diffusion of networked electricity shifted the American economy into a higher gear. This transformation took decades, but the end result was a far more productive economy. Today it is difficult to imagine a world without networked electricity, given the importance it plays in our lives. In much the same way, new information and communications technologies are in the process of transforming our economic system.

What is the potential catalyst that could trigger an upsurge in U.S. productivity growth as it is traditionally measured? Researchers at McKinsey & Company may have the answer. They argue that we are on the cusp of unprecedented changes in what they call "the economics of interaction." The term may be unfamiliar, but we all have experience with it. Interactions encompass the searching, coordinating, and monitoring that people and firms do when they exchange goods, services, or ideas. Interactions permeate every economy, big and small, developed or developing. According to researchers at McKinsey, interactions account for a huge share of U.S. economic activity, about one third of total GDP—or a whopping $2.5 trillion.

To understand the importance of interactions in our

economy, consider how much time employees have to spend at work communicating with suppliers, clients, and other employees to do their jobs. Or consider how much time workers spend collecting data and doing collaborative problem solving on the job. Interactions are a vital part of the service sector in America, which is by far the largest sector of the economy. Many of us take for granted today how easy it is to track down an order or collect some data for a project we are working on. Several decades ago, great effort was expended on such activity, but this is no longer true today.

Our ability to manipulate and process data has thus far outstripped our ability to communicate and interact. The limited ability to communicate has impeded our ability to interact more efficiently in the past. But this state of affairs seems destined to change soon. New networking capabilities are moving out of research-and-development labs and are becoming part of the nation's communications infrastructure. The build-out of this infrastructure will dramatically transform and enhance the carrying capacity of our networks. As the McKinsey researchers point out, these innovative forces herald a new age of abundant interactive capability.

If McKinsey's research is on target, as we believe, the coming new age of abundant interactive capability could lead to a huge productivity dividend in the years ahead. Many economists will tell you that there has been little or no improvement in service sector productivity—a sector that accounts today for nearly three quarters of total economic activity and employment in America. But the service sector could be increasingly transformed by innovations in information and communications technologies. In the near future,

McKinsey researchers believe, workers engaged primarily in interactive activities could do their jobs in less than half of the time they currently spend. For the U.S. economy, such savings could translate into productivity gains worth over $1 trillion, or one seventh of the nation's total output of goods and services.

Corporations are also likely to find new ways of organizing their businesses more efficiently. Introducing new information and communications technologies into an existing business structure is by no means a surefire strategy to achieve higher levels of productivity, as many CEOs can attest. Adopting new technology requires a good deal of what management gurus call business process reengineering. Essentially, this encompasses finding the most efficient ways of utilizing new information and communications technologies to raise efficiency and profitability. Given the quickening pace of technological change, this is no easy feat. Recent experience shows that it often requires painful restructuring. But such measures are necessary to reap the full benefits of new information and communications technologies.

There are thousands of examples of how corporations are working overtime to find more efficient ways of doing business. Jack Welch, CEO of General Electric, notes that the railroad companies have so dramatically improved their efficiency by employing modern information systems that they need only about half as many cars as before to carry an equivalent amount of freight. According to experts in the steel industry, computers have changed what they make and how they make it. They also have changed how they make the equipment needed to make the steel. As this case illustrates, entirely new corporate structures will emerge from re-thinking how to best incorporate new technologies into an organization.

Microsoft CEO Bill Gates envisions a "frictionless" economy, an economy where lower searching and communication costs lead to more efficient market mechanisms for exchanging goods and services. What would a "frictionless" economy look like? Think for a moment about a company such as Amazon.com. Incorporated only a couple of years ago, Amazon.com today advertises itself as the world's largest bookstore. Unlike conventional booksellers, Amazon has no physical stores and relatively few employees. Amazon offers customers discounts on all of its 2.5 million titles. Despite its lack of physical presence, the firm is able to serve customers from all over the world fast and efficiently. Amazon continually strives to harness the ever-rising power and intelligence of information technology to make shopping more pleasurable for its fast-growing list of customers.

For companies like Amazon.com today and countless others in the future, the technology revolution will make it easy to reach new customers anywhere in the world, anytime. Communication with customers, whether in the form of advertising, research, or marketing, is likely to shift from broadcasting (one-to-many) to narrowcasting (one-to-one) as the cost of interacting with current and prospective customers declines. The enhanced interactive capabilities made possible by computing and communications technologies are destined to spur revolutionary changes in how businesses interact with customers.

Just as it would have been difficult to overstate the importance of the railroad boom to the American economy in the nineteenth century, we think it will be difficult to overstate the importance of the Internet boom to the global economy in the first few decades of the twenty-first century. Those who dismiss recent excitement about the Internet as mere hype would do well to listen to Intel's CEO, Andrew Grove, who is well positioned to understand both the science and the economics causing that excitement.

According to Grove, "The Internet is like a twenty-foot tidal wave coming thousands of miles across the Pacific, and we are in kayaks. It's been coming across the Pacific for thousands of miles and gaining momentum, and it's going to lift you and drop you. . . . It affects everybody—the computer industry, telecommunications, the media, chip makers, and the software world. Some are more aware of this than others."

A similar view comes from John Chambers, president of Cisco Systems, which makes the routers and switches that connect the Internet around the world. Described by the *New York Times* as leader of "the most important American company no one has ever heard of," Chambers's rhetoric tops that of Intel's Grove. "What people have not grasped is that the Internet will change everything. . . . The industrial revolution brought together people with machines in factories, and the Internet revolution will bring together people with knowledge and information in virtual companies. And it will have every bit as much impact as the industrial revolution. It will promote globalization at an incredible pace. But instead of happening over 100 years, like the industrial revolution, it will happen over 7 years."

It is clear that the most successful entrepreneur of the information age, Bill Gates, agrees with these assessments. Microsoft's CEO has recently refocused the entire energy of his giant corporation to accommodate the new advances in computer networks, whose importance he had not anticipated in the original edition of his 1995 book *The Road Ahead*. There will undoubtedly be investment excesses and colossal corporate missteps as the Internet boom proceeds. Judging from the astronomical valuations now put on many Internet-related stocks, there is no doubt that financial markets now view the Internet as the next big thing.

IT'S LIFE, JIM, BUT NOT AS WE KNOW IT

The rapid growth of the Internet has made many Americans increasingly aware of the potential for the information technology revolution to transform the economy. In the meantime, another revolution is brewing in the life sciences, one that also has its roots in quantum physics and the laws of the microcosm. It is still early, but scientists tell us that the accelerating pace of innovation in the life sciences could result in truly stunning advances in biology and medicine that should have a profound impact on the lives of boomers and non-boomers alike. The recent news that scientists have been able to clone sheep and other mammals seems certain to be followed by more sensational breakthroughs over the next several decades.

At the foundation of the coming revolution in the life sciences is the convergence of information technology, biology, and medicine. Computers are allowing researchers to explore the depths of our cells and decode the secrets of life. Scientists today confidently predict that by the year 2005 they will have a complete map of every gene in the human body (estimated to be roughly 100,000 genes). Not long ago, even dreaming about such an achievement would have been dismissed as fanciful. But scientists associated with the federally funded Human Genome Project now believe that the mapping process may wrap up before the year 2005.

Scientists' ability to decode the secrets of life is increasing on a par with the power of computer chips. The number of DNA sequences that scientists can identify doubles roughly every two years. The task of mapping the human genome is daunting because there are a hundred thousand genes hidden among twenty-three pairs of chromosomes in our cells. Genes can be viewed essentially as long strings of letters, which scientists have designated A, T, G, and C. The human genome is composed of some three billion such letters. To put this in perspective, if we printed out the entire human genome, it would fill a thousand Manhattan telephone books.

A complete mapping of the entire human genome is likely to lay the foundation for a new era in the treatment of disease. Defects in our genes are responsible for cystic fibrosis, muscular dystrophy, and nearly four thousand other hereditary diseases. Moreover, altered genes are known to play a part in cancer, heart disease, diabetes, and many other common diseases that afflict us. Scientists know that genetic alterations increase a person's risk of developing a disorder, and they understand that disease itself results from the interaction of genetic factors and environmental factors, including diet and lifestyle.

By unlocking the code of life, scientists will shift from

finding genes—which will then simply be a matter of scanning a computer database—to understanding them. Major improvements in the early detection and treatment of disease and new approaches to prevention should be an early dividend of an improved understanding of the genetic basis of life. Scientists tell us that once the molecular basis of a disease has been uncovered, they have a far better chance of defeating it. James Watson, discoverer of the helical structure of the DNA molecule with Francis Crick, once remarked that we used to think our future was in the stars, but now we know it's in our genes. Drugs discovered with the information derived from the Human Genome Project could one day be used to cure many of the life-threatening diseases that afflict people today. Additionally, the new discoveries associated with unlocking the code of life could fundamentally alter the aging process.

Breakthroughs in medicine and basic biology are yielding important insights into the nature of aging. As author Carol Orlock observes, new theories and discoveries are opening up wellsprings of information about how aging occurs, why it happens, and what might be done about it. Scientists recently succeeded for the first time in extending the life of cells grown in a test tube. Physicians now talk about the possibility of taking a person's damaged cells, manipulating and repairing them, and giving them back to the same patient. This could revolutionize, among other things, treatment for burn victims. Whether scientists have discovered a cellular fountain of youth is still open to question, but the potential for current genetic research to yield major medical advances is not.

If there is anything we can say with certainty about the

coming revolution in the life sciences, it is that predictions about the impossibility of certain advances in the future will turn out to be incorrect. History supports this contention. In 1935 scientists stated that understanding the true nature of the gene was beyond humankind's capabilities. In 1974 they said it was impossible to determine the complete sequence of the human genome. Ten years later scientists said it was impossible to alter specific genes within the embryo. In 1996 they said it was impossible to clone people from adult cells. No credible scientist would make any of these claims today.

The revolution in information technology has played a major role in shaping a new age in medicine and the drug discovery process. Computer chips are playing an increasingly larger role in biotechnology and the development of new and more powerful medicines. The science of applying chip technology to medicine has been dubbed "robochemistry." In the past, pharmaceutical companies employed hundreds of researchers in the hope of generating twenty-five to fifty molecules a year that would be candidates as potential drugs. With the advent of more powerful information technology, pharmaceuticals executives today talk of creating thousands or perhaps millions of test molecules. The end result is likely to be better and more cost-effective treatments for a wide array of illnesses such as arthritis, cancer, and Alzheimer's disease, to name a few.

As seventy-six million baby boomers continue to age, there will be an enormous demand for new medical technologies to help the boomers live healthier and longer lives. If this demand intersects with a bumper crop of new medi-

FIGURE 4. UNLOCKING THE CODE OF LIFE

Number of Genes Discovered by the Human Genome Project

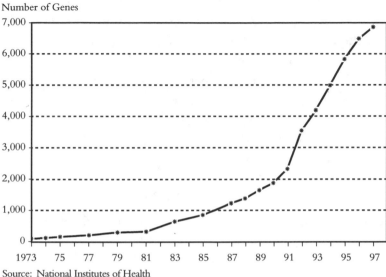

Source: National Institutes of Health

cines and new ways to diagnose and treat diseases, as seems likely, life expectancy could rise far more rapidly than currently expected. In this way, advances in the life sciences will have a major impact on America's demographic profile in the future. The good news is that we may all end up living longer, healthier lives. The challenge will be figuring out how to pay for that privilege, individually and collectively. We will return to that topic later when we consider financial scenarios for the boomers' retirement years.

If the Internet has already become the next big thing, the life sciences revolution certainly appears well positioned to become the *next* next big thing. Consider Figure 4, which shows the exponential progress in the number of human genes that have been identified. Looking at such data, our impression is that the biotech industry is roughly at the same point of development as the semiconductor industry was during the early 1970s, when Intel was coming out with its first chips for use in handheld calculators. We suspect that something like Moore's Law will begin to hold true in the biotech industry. In this sense, investors may be close to being present at the creation of what is likely to become one of the most important industries of the next century.

MAY YOU LIVE IN INTERESTING TIMES

We believe that the ongoing convergence of information and communications technology carries with it the promise of better economic times, especially against the backdrop of benign demographic trends during America's Prime Time. In our view, a powerful surge in the U.S. economy's interactive capability is likely to deliver a meaningful productivity dividend in the years ahead. If we are right, the future economic payoff from the revolution in information and communications technologies could be far larger than most people imagine.

Even modest-sounding increases in the nation's rate of annual productivity growth would have major implications for the standard of living baby boomers are likely to enjoy during their retirement years. For example, annual growth in output per worker over the last seventy-five years averaged 2.3 percent. In contrast, it averaged only 1.2 percent in the 1970–1990 period. If productivity growth merely picked up to its long-term average rate of 2.3 percent, average take-home pay per worker should rise by roughly 70 percent by the year 2020. As economist Paul Krugman notes, "Productivity isn't everything, but in the long run it is almost everything."

Faster productivity growth would not guarantee low inflation and interest rates, but would certainly help make the Federal Reserve's job of maintaining price stability much easier. That's because faster productivity growth would increase the Fed's estimate of the economy's "speed limit," or rate of growth that can be sustained without triggering inflation. With faster productivity growth, the Fed should be able to pursue a kinder, gentler monetary policy that would encourage rapid growth with fewer worries about inflation.

A productivity boom could also promote lower interest by reducing firms' need for capital financing. If new technologies such as the Internet permit firms to do business with less inventory and less money tied up in bricks and mortar, a reduced demand for capital should permit interest rates to decline. In fact, it is notable that many of the most successful firms of the information age have relatively little need to tap the capital markets for additional financing once their own cash flow becomes established. Microsoft, for example, has been notable by its absence from the capital markets after its initial public offering raised $58.7 million in 1986.

If the technology revolution keeps the price of capital goods dropping, firms will simply get more bang for their buck as they invest in their business, which lessens the need for borrowing and reduces pressure on interest rates. We will explore this later, but this scenario suggests further impressive gains in the stock market during America's Prime Time, from what is already a lofty valuation level.

Even if the technology revolution brings many benefits to the American economy, it also calls to mind the old Chinese curse: "May you live in interesting times." Clearly an acceleration of productivity growth will not be painless. As economist Joseph Schumpeter first noted, the interaction of capitalism and technological change is a process of "creative destruction," whereby old jobs are eliminated even as many new jobs are created. If the technology revolution unfolds as we expect, the already rapid pace of creative destruction in America's economy is likely to accelerate further in coming years. That means the idea of lifetime jobs, or even lifetime careers, will lose relevance as new products and services come and go with increasing frequency.

Faster product cycles bring more rapid job changes and speed up the process by which large and small firms rise and fall. In addition, most economists believe that the widening gap between rich and poor in recent years has more to do with the technology revolution than with competition from low-wage labor overseas. The challenge for America's policy makers will be to rethink income security, health care, and pension policies that were designed for an era when a large fraction of the workforce enjoyed something akin to lifetime employment. That era has gone the way of Ozzie and Harriet. To thrive in the high-tech era, American workers will need new forms of income security and portable health and pension plans, instead of benefits that are terminated when workers are between jobs.

If demographics and the technology revolution were the only major forces at work during America's Prime Time, we would still draw positive conclusions about prospects for low inflation, low interest rates, and buoyant financial markets. But there is another powerful force pointing in the same direction: the impact of global markets on the American economy. Global economic integration has been a fact of life throughout the baby boomers' adult years, and the forces of globalization are likely to become even stronger as the boomers move through the prime of life and on toward retirement.

3

Globalization: The Golden Age of Market Capitalism?

JUST IN TIME for many baby boomers to enter their fifth decade, the world economy entered one of the most wrenching periods of change in history. The major catalyst for this historic change was the disintegration of the Soviet Union and the collapse of Communism in the late 1980s. This extraordinary event had major implications for the global balance of power, effectively leaving America as the sole remaining military superpower. Also, the collapse of what was once thought to be the world's third-largest economy effectively leaves market-based capitalism as the sole remaining economic ideology.

When Germans danced amidst the rubble of the Berlin Wall in 1989, few could have anticipated the major changes to the global economy that would eventually follow. But it is now clear that the collapse of central planning as a viable economic ideology has prompted a revolution in economic policy making from Latin America to Eastern Europe, India, China, and even Vietnam. Even Japan is undergoing its own painful form of economic perestroika as it tries to reform a system described by investment strategist Brian Reading as "not capitalism with warts, but communism with beauty spots." Many of these reforms are still in their early stages. Despite recent turbulence in the developing economies, the reintegration of the former Communist countries into the global economy arguably has set the stage for a new golden age of capitalism, with America well positioned to play a leading role.

INTEGRATION, DISINTEGRATION, AND REINTEGRATION

The increasing integration of the world economy is not new. In recent decades it can be seen as a resumption of a trend that began in the mid–nineteenth century and ended with World War I. During that period, there were few artificial barriers to the exchange of goods and money among countries. The flows of products and financial capital across national borders were relatively large. For example, world exports of goods and services were 9.8 percent of world GDP in 1880. By 1913, the export share of world GDP had risen to 11.9 percent.

As integration deepened, there was a marked convergence in living standards across countries, and an improvement in all of those standards. The process of globalization was then disrupted by the two world wars. The period encompassing the war years saw a marked decline in globalization as economic cooperation among nations plummeted. By 1950, world exports had fallen to 7.1 percent of world GDP, far below the level reached in 1913.

Since the end of World War II, the world has resumed the trend toward integration. By 1990, world exports of goods and services had risen to 17.1 percent of world GDP—the highest level ever recorded during the past two centuries. And this was before the collapse of Communism heralded an even greater expansion of global economic integration.

The boomer generation faces a more intense phase of globalization for a simple reason: Virtually the entire world has now embraced one form of capitalism or another. As one wag recently noted, the only people who no longer believe in the efficiency of free markets are the Cubans, the North Koreans, and active fund managers who think they can outperform the stock market.

ECONOMIC SHOCK WAVES FROM THE COLLAPSE OF COMMUNISM

Prior to the collapse of Communism, what most of us thought of as the "global economy" was not actually global. For practical reasons, our focus during the cold war was on the *non-Communist, nonsocialist* world, which had relatively open borders and a common, if uneven, commitment to free market principles. That "global economy" consisted of roughly 1.2 billion people—800 million in the twenty-five industrial countries and another 400 million living in a dozen less developed satellite economies.

With statues of Lenin having fallen like graven images, we

are now witnessing the emergence of a truly global economy. The new global economy includes nearly the entire population of the world, or roughly 5.7 billion people. In other words, almost 80 percent of mankind, or about 4.5 billion people, are attempting to reenter the global marketplace after years of isolation. Put differently, it's as if 4.5 billion people have just been let out of jail. They now need new jobs and modern technology to bring their living standards in line with the 1.2 billion who have enjoyed greater prosperity under capitalism.

This may be overstating the case, but only by a bit. Some Communist nations, like China, have been moving toward capitalism since the late 1970s. And in other highly controlled economies, like India's, policy makers are talking a great deal about free markets but are taking their time in implementing reforms. However, the general direction is clear: A truly global economy is developing. Compared to their parents, America's baby boomers face greater economic opportunities—and greater risks—as this more intense phase of globalization proceeds.

Formerly Communist and socialist nations are putting their economies through wrenching changes for one major reason: to improve their own living standards. To do so, they need access to financial capital, modern telecommunications and computing equipment, and a wide range of expensive equipment ranging from tractors to power turbines. To participate in global capital markets, they need technical assistance to deal with a bewildering array of "new" problems. For example: How should new corporate or government bond markets be structured? How should companies' finan-

FIGURE 5. GOING GLOBAL

World Trade and Real GDP

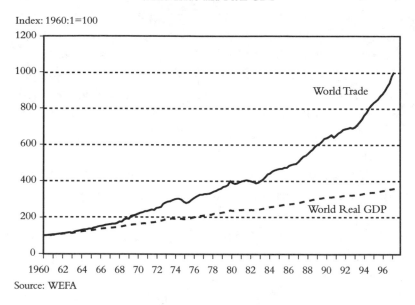

Source: WEFA

cial statements be prepared to meet internationally accepted accounting standards?

WHY AMERICA BENEFITS FROM GLOBALIZATION

Virtually all economists agree that expanding international trade has had a positive impact on living standards around the world in recent decades, even though trade has contributed to some increase in wage inequality and to sharp dislocations in various industries from time to time. Data shows that total trade has long tended to grow faster than the overall world economy. This trend is illustrated clearly for the major industrial nations in Figure 5.

In our opinion, America is extremely well positioned to benefit from the latest wave of globalization for several reasons. First, in many of the areas just mentioned, American firms have a strong comparative advantage and are considered representative of "best practices" in a global context. General Electric, for example, dominates many of the industries it operates in, from power-generation equipment to aircraft engines, medical imaging systems, and engineered plastics, and has become an export powerhouse selling its products in every corner of the globe. Led by companies such as General Electric, America now sends about 35 percent of its production of tradable goods to foreign markets, up from only 9 percent in 1950. Likewise, more than 25 percent of America's corporate profits now originate in overseas markets, compared to a mere 7 percent in 1948.

Second, American firms such as Microsoft and Intel are dominating the information revolution and have acquired near-monopoly power in core technologies of operating systems and high-end microprocessors. Likewise, the Internet is an American invention that is making the entire world increasingly dependent on communications standards and protocols developed largely in America. As the explosive growth in Microsoft's profits has demonstrated, controlling standards is enormously valuable in the information age.

What is true for computer operating systems is also true for other types of capitalist "software," such as accounting standards or rules for listing a company's stock on the New York Stock Exchange. American firms' mastery and control of such rules and standards has made New York the preferred location for many global financial transactions, boosting the fortunes of the nation's banks, securities houses, and accounting firms. Ironically, American dominance of international financial transactions has come despite the nation's low savings rate and its chronic dependence on foreign money to finance large trade deficits.

Not incidentally, America's dominance in many high-tech fields has cemented the role of English as the lingua franca of the business world, which is a substantial competitive advantage in many fields. This advantage may eventually fade as automated translation systems become more sophisticated over the next few decades. But we expect the English-language edge to remain important for at least the next five to ten years—that is, during America's Prime Time.

Third, U.S. firms have responded quickly to rapidly changing markets thanks to the flexibility and openness of the American economic system. This flexibility is especially evident in the labor market, which has fostered a net gain of more than twenty-five million new jobs between 1980 and 1995. That compares to a net gain of only four million new jobs over the same period in continental Europe, despite the region's somewhat larger economy and workforce. Many analysts believe that this simply reflects declining U.S. wages. However, as economist Horace W. Brock points out, when inflation is properly measured, the average worker's real income actually rose by 30 percent during the period. Instead, the dynamic job growth reflects the nation's entrepreneurial climate and flexible capital markets.

As Brock observes, America has developed an impressive

network of venture capitalists and investment bankers who earn exceptional profits by funding entrepreneurs. In 1995 alone, for example, American firms raised $29 billion through new stock issues known as initial public offerings, or IPOs. In contrast, in the entire 1975–1979 period, the total volume of IPOs was only $1.35 billion. Brock estimates that 80 to 90 percent of funds raised by venture capitalists or investment bankers go toward hiring people, so that investing is becoming indistinguishable from hiring. America's competitors in Europe and Japan are by and large still struggling to create equally dynamic ways to fund new ventures and create new jobs.

Consider a shortlist of U.S. companies that did not exist in 1975 but which have gone on to become multibillion-dollar companies and household names in the last two decades: Amgen, Cisco Systems, Compaq, Federal Express, The Gap, Home Depot, Microsoft, Oracle, Staples, and Toys "R" Us. Such companies have become major employers by developing new technologies themselves, or by rapidly exploiting new technologies. To be sure, these high-growth companies may have put other companies out of business and eliminated jobs in the process. Nevertheless, the evidence clearly shows that far more jobs have been created than eliminated in recent decades.

The numbers are startling. As mentioned above, America created twenty-five million new jobs between 1980 and 1995 on a *net* basis. But that was the result of a period of economic transformation that saw the elimination of forty-two million jobs and the creation of sixty-seven million jobs. As economist Brock points out, "The nation that fired the most hired the most," reflecting the process of "creative destruction" permitted by America's dynamic and intensely competitive version of capitalism.

GLOBAL COMPETITION IN THE INFORMATION AGE

It is becoming increasingly clear to business leaders in Europe, Japan, and the developing nations that their own economic systems will need to become more dynamic and entrepreneurial to remain competitive in the information age. In turn, this is creating new opportunities for American firms to expand their overseas operations and gain valuable market share. In Japan, for example, the gradual opening of financial markets has provided opportunities for America's financial powerhouses, such as Goldman Sachs and Merrill Lynch, to become increasingly dominant forces in local markets, displacing major Japanese firms in the process. A similar trend in the field of financial services has been evident in Europe and in the developing economies as well.

As Damon Runyon once observed, "It may be that the race is not always to the swift, nor the battle to the strong—but that's the way to bet." If the technology revolution has accelerated the clock speed of the global economy, in one industry after another there are likely to be strategic first-mover advantages that reward the most nimble competitors. Just as England enjoyed a long period of competitive dominance after it gave birth to the industrial revolution more than two hundred years ago, America could be likewise favored, thanks to its leading role in the information revolution.

For many of America's commercial competitors, this unpleasant prospect is creating furious efforts to reform their economies and catch up. But as economist Brock observes, this is not easy for cultures that could not imagine putting large amounts of capital at the disposal of twenty-seven-year-old immigrants, even if they happen to have good ideas and persuasive business plans. Traditional bank-based financial systems are far more comfortable funding well-connected fifty-year-olds working for blue-chip companies than they are placing money with young people.

Brock points out that the information revolution places a premium on abstract fields, which are typically the province of young people. These include "software design, proof theory, digital circuit design, artificial intelligence, Bayesian pattern recognition theory, object-oriented design of software interfaces, optimal control theory, encryption logic, distributed computing theory, packet-switching algorithms, Boolean algebra, information theory, [and] automata theory, to cite a few."

Funding entrepreneurs with expertise in such fields is important, and will require cultural changes in foreign corporate structures and financial market practices that will not come easily. For this reason, we expect many foreign competitors to fall back to the time-honored strategic position "If you can't beat them, join them." This should open the door to numerous joint ventures and strategic alliances that are likely to be conducted on terms favorable to U.S. firms. Accordingly, we expect America's competitive lead in the information age to persist for some time, leaving the nation well positioned to benefit from globalization. For the nation's competitors, concern is mounting that humorist Lewis Grizzard's words will be prophetic. "Life is like a dog sled," said Grizzard, "and if you're not the lead dog, the view never changes."

GLOBALIZATION AND
THE FINANCIAL MARKETS

Globalization has been extraordinarily kind to U.S. financial markets in recent years. Consider, for example, how the U.S. managed to enjoy an investment boom in the 1990s despite its low savings rate. As we discussed earlier, part of the story is that firms have received more bang for their investment buck thanks to the technology revolution and falling prices of investment goods. That said, the nation has also financed much of its investment the old-fashioned way: by borrowing from foreigners.

Reflecting America's dependence on foreign money, foreign holdings of total privately held U.S. public debt have mushroomed in the 1990s, from 20 percent at the beginning of the decade to nearly 38 percent in the fourth quarter of 1997. The U.S. Department of the Treasury estimates foreign holdings of U.S. government debt at a whopping $1.3 trillion. Like Blanche DuBois in *A Streetcar Named Desire*, as a nation we have become increasingly dependent on the kindness of strangers. Accordingly, one of the biggest risks to our positive scenario for America's Prime Time is a U.S. balance-of-payments crisis if there is some shock overseas—for example, a huge earthquake in Tokyo or a complete meltdown of Asia's financial system—that severely disrupts foreign money flows to the United States.

During the past two decades, cross-border transactions in total bonds and equities have grown explosively as various restrictions to such transactions have been lifted. In the United States and most other advanced economies around the world, such transactions have expanded from less than 10 percent of GDP in the early 1980s to over 100 percent of GDP in the 1990s. The influence of advances in information and communications technologies is also clearly evident in global currency markets. Daily volumes in the world's foreign exchange markets now exceed $1 trillion. New York has become the hub of many of these transactions, and the American economy has benefited substantially as thousands of traders— described by author Tom Wolfe as "masters of the universe"—have taken out tiny crumbs of commissions on each and every transaction.

The collapse of Communism has also boosted the U.S. stock market by raising the value of American firms with global franchises. Brand names such as Coca-Cola, Gillette, and Microsoft are no longer confined to the developed nations and are rapidly becoming global household words in a brave new world of 5.7 billion consumers. Likewise, American financial powerhouses such as Citicorp, J. P. Morgan, Merrill Lynch, Morgan Stanley, and Goldman Sachs have extended their reach throughout the developed world and emerging markets alike in response to explosive growth in cross-border money flows. Just as stars like Madonna and Michael Jackson can now make tens of millions of dollars by selling their songs to a global marketplace, America's corporate stars now have far greater opportunities to market their products globally than anyone dreamed of ten years ago.

FIGURE 6. THE TWILIGHT OF INFLATION

G-7 Nations Consumer Price Inflation

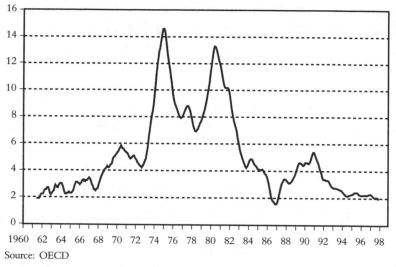

Percent Change from Previous Year

Source: OECD

The end of the cold war has also boosted financial markets in the 1990s by creating deflationary pressures that helped bring down interest rates around the world. In a classic study of interest rates over forty centuries, *A History of Interest Rates,* bond analyst Sidney Homer found that peacetime conditions have typically been most conducive to low inflation and low interest rates. With the end of the cold war, the United States and other major industrial nations have been able to cut defense budgets sharply and reduce overall deficit spending. That has undoubtedly helped bring bond yields down during the 1990s, making stocks relatively more attractive in the process.

We agree with Sidney Homer that the long-run outlook for interest rates depends critically on prospects for war or peace. As Homer and coauthor Richard Johannesen noted in 1969, "Those who are attempting a long-range forecast of interest rates probably should always ask themselves first of all: 'Is the outlook for more war or more peace?' If the answer is 'more war,' then more inflation and high interest rates seem inevitable until we reach the point of wartime controls. If the answer is 'more peace,' then less inflation, and stable-to-lower interest rates seem likely."

The collapse of Communism has created an environment that should make it relatively easy for central banks to keep inflation low over the next decade. Put simply, the arrival of billions of new entrants to the global economy represents a huge increase in the supply of labor. That should help restrain labor cost growth in the high-wage nations. Labor accounts for roughly two thirds of total production costs in industrial economies, making such costs critical to the overall inflation process. With wages in many areas of the developing nations still well below ten dollars per day, there is effectively a large reserve army of the underpaid to keep wage pressures muted in the high-wage nations, especially for unskilled labor.

Historically, financial markets have usually boomed during periods of disinflation, when inflation rates decline gradually. In that sense, the deflationary impact of the collapse of Communism has been an important aspect of the bull market in U.S. stocks in the 1990s. Currently there is every indication that formerly Communist and socialist nations will continue to make their presence felt in global markets over the coming decade. That should bring increasing supplies of goods, services, and labor to the United States and other high-cost nations, creating further downward pressure on inflation.

As Sidney Homer noted, "Almost every generation is eventually shocked by the behavior of interest rates, because, in fact, market rates of interest in modern times have rarely been stable for long. Usually they are rising or falling to unexpected extremes." Something similar could be said for stock market valuations, and we will return to that subject in Part III. In our judgment, the combined effects of globalization, technology, and baby boomer demographics all point in the direction of shockingly low interest rates—and shockingly high stock market valuations—at least until the baby boomers retire.

THE DARK SIDE OF THE FORCE

Without a doubt, America's financial markets and the investing public have benefited enormously from globalization in recent decades. We would also argue that America's standard of living, on average, has received an enormous boost from globalization. The same statements can be made, perhaps even more strongly, about the effects of the technology revolution. This is not to say, however, that all Americans have benefited equally. If anything, we are reminded of the old story of the statistician whose head was in a freezer while his feet were in an oven. On average, he felt just fine.

The biggest concern about the impact of globalization

on the economy was highlighted by Douglas Coupland's controversial novel *Generation X*, about young Americans born in the late sixties and early seventies. Published during the recession of 1991, Coupland portrays a generation with nothing to look forward to except a "McJob," referring to a low-paying, zero-prestige, no-benefits-package job in the service industry. Coupland also coined the term "Brazilification" to refer to the widening gap between the rich and poor and the gradual disappearance of the middle class.

Coupland's grim vision may seem a bit dated in the late 1990s. Along with a much-improved job market, consumer confidence has recovered to levels not seen since the go-go 1960s. But Coupland's underlying concern about a widening gap between the rich and the poor is echoed by almost anyone who has looked at the numbers—or out their car window. Over the last two decades, employment trends have been far less favorable for less-skilled workers. According to Princeton University economist Alan Krueger, the wages of workers with high school degrees have failed to keep pace with those of workers with college degrees, resulting in sharp disparities in pay. In 1980, for example, college graduates typically earned 40 percent more than high school graduates. By 1994, college graduates earned 78 percent more than high school graduates. Krueger also estimates that real family income fell by roughly 10 percent between 1979 and 1996 for families in the bottom fifth of the income distribution, compared to an average gain of 28 percent for families in the top fifth.

Is globalization to blame for the rise in income inequality?

The answer is a tricky "yes, but . . ." Yes, globalization is partly to blame, but other factors, such as the technology revolution, appear to be far more important. For example, Krueger estimates that the expansion of computer use can account for one third to two thirds of the increased payoff of education in recent years, which suggests increasingly important distinctions between the information haves and information have-nots. According to a survey of economists conducted in 1995 at a Federal Reserve conference on wage inequality, technology was seen to account for 44 percent of the rise in wage inequality, with trade a distant second place at 11 percent. That also squares with several careful studies that tried to measure the impact of trade on wages, taking into account the fact that roughly 90 percent of the American economy is still domestically focused.

That said, Krueger and other economists expect that trade will place greater pressure on less-skilled workers in the future. The reason is that there are a great many unskilled workers in the world who earn very little. As Krueger notes, there are 1.5 billion potential workers who have left school before they reached age thirteen. And half the world's population leaves school at age sixteen or earlier. As global economic integration increasingly places America's less-skilled workers in competition with hordes of low-paid workers overseas—or in competition with cheap robots—the result is likely to be even more wage inequality.

Even if the twin forces of technology and globalization continue to make America's Prime Time a golden age for investors, it will not be a golden age for market capitalism unless we also deal constructively with the dark side of the force.

Under current trends, "Brazilification" of the economy seems likely to continue, if not accelerate, during America's Prime Time. If not addressed soon, the political and economic consequences could be increasingly serious during the Big Chill, when other forces point toward intense political polarization and turbulence.

Part II

THE BIG CHILL

Welcome to my nightmare.
—*ALICE COOPER*

FROM A DEMOGRAPHIC perspective, we have argued that there are plenty of reasons to be optimistic about the economy in the next decade. As surely as muscle turns to fat, the baby boom generation will be getting older, but not yet *old*. As the center of gravity of the population moves through its productive middle-aged years and its peak years of earning and saving, the overall economic impact should be benign. And if Aristotle was right to celebrate the wisdom and even temper of men at their prime, we may look forward to a relatively placid political environment as the baby boomers pass through their middle years.

But we want to look ahead even further, to that period when the baby boomers enter old age en masse. That will begin in earnest in 2011, when the baby boomers born in 1946 turn sixty-five and become eligible for Social Security benefits. The retirement wave will continue through the early 2030s, when the back-end boomers become eligible for Social Security—or what's left of it. The timing of the retirement wave for the back-end boomers is tougher to forecast because it is highly likely that the younger boomers will have to wait until they are seventy or older to begin collecting retirement benefits.

Most Americans appear to have a sense that there will be economic problems when the boomers retire in large numbers. There have been enough reports in the media about looming financial problems for Social Security that the public is aware of a general problem. That said, there also appears to be a fair degree of complacency that, somehow, the problem will be fixed.

In contrast, expert opinion on Social Security and related demographic issues is, to put it mildly, more pessimistic. As we will discuss, those who run the numbers carefully are nearly apocalyptic about the boomers' retirement years. Couched in the careful language of academic studies, economists who have studied these issues carefully are essentially predicting a severe and potentially devastating financial crisis sometime during the boomers' retirement years *if nothing is done soon.*

Naturally, if severe economic problems surface during the boomers' not-so-golden years, acute political problems are likely as well. Many economists warn of coming generational warfare as the boomers try to saddle younger generations with massive retirement bills. Those warnings appear well founded, because punitive tax rates on younger workers will be needed if numerous retired boomers insist on generous retirement programs. If the boomers are to be supported as generously as their parents, some analysts estimate, net taxes of around *80 percent of total earnings* will be necessary on remaining workers.

Moreover, as fiscal pressures mount we would not be surprised to see bitter *intra*generational warfare, pitting boomer versus boomer. That would oppose the interests of the vast majority of boomers who retire with insufficient savings to the interests of the wealthy minority—today's "gold collar" workers—who will retire with ample savings. Not only are wealthy boomers likely to receive extremely low returns from the Social Security and Medicare programs they have funded, they are also liable to become targets of punitive wealth taxes—that is, taxes on their accumulated financial assets or real estate holdings. So if you think American politics are polarized now, wait until the year 2025.

French philosopher Michel de Montaigne had this to say about the elderly, writing after he had reached old age: "We do not so much give up our vices as change them, and in my opinion for the worse. Besides a foolish and tottering pride, a tedious garrulity, prickly and unsociable moods, and an absurd preoccupation with money after we have lost the use for it, I find old age an increase of envy, injustice, and malice. It stamps more wrinkles on our minds than on our faces, and seldom, or very rarely, does one find souls that do not acquire, as they age, a sour and musty smell."

We are not trying to become targets for hate mail from the AARP. Please direct such correspondence to Montaigne.

We ourselves are hoping to grow old gracefully, as many do successfully. But we are also trying to be realistic, and we see many reasons why the politics of our retirement years are likely to be far more cantankerous—and upsetting to financial markets—than those of our middle years. If we add to the picture the dark side of the technology revolution and globalization, including accelerated destruction (and creation) of jobs and widening gaps between the haves and the have-nots, our scenario verges on *Blade Runner Meets Grumpy Old Men*.

Get ready for the Big Chill.

4

The Coming Crunch in Residential Real Estate: Who Will Buy the Boomers' Homes?

WHEN PETER, PAUL, and Mary made fun in the 1960s of all the ticky-tacky little boxes that were scattered on hillsides, few would have predicted how valuable those little boxes would become in the 1970s and 1980s. With hindsight, however, it was inevitable that when the hordes of baby boomers hit the housing market housing prices would get pushed up dramatically.

For the parents of the baby boomers, who borrowed prodigiously to achieve the dream of home ownership, the great real estate inflation of the 1970s and 1980s created a financial windfall. Not only did their homes rise in value far more than most expected, but their mortgages turned out to be remarkably easy to service as well. The reason is simple: A surge in inflation is typically great for debtors because they can pay back their debts in cheaper dollars.

The parents of the boomers also benefited from generous

tax deductions for payment of mortgage interest that were put in place to encourage home ownership, and which were spectacularly successful in doing so. All of these circumstances combined to create a cult of home ownership as not just a lifestyle decision but also a surefire investment. Having had a terrific ride on the real estate market themselves, parents of baby boomers were quick to encourage their children as young adults to get in the game early on.

For the front-end boomers, who got there ahead of the rest of the pack, that was generally good advice. As we discussed earlier, it was the front-end boomers who were well positioned to buy starter homes in the 1970s, trade up to bigger homes in the early 1980s, and ride a wave of demand for housing created by their numerous younger siblings and relatives. It all worked very well until the late 1980s, when the game of musical chairs stopped.

THE DAY THE MUSIC DIED

Both commercial borrowers and residential mortgage holders got hit hard in the late 1980s when the Federal Reserve Board raised interest rates to cope with building inflationary pressures. As the economy slowed and debt servicing burdens mounted, both commercial and residential real estate markets slumped badly. Especially hard hit in the early 1990s were regions that earlier had been overheated, such as New England and California. The savings and loan crisis, which had been brewing for years, also came to a head in the early 1990s, creating a public furor about reckless real estate lending that had a chilling effect on both borrowers and lenders.

Cutbacks in defense spending in the early 1990s were especially painful for New England and southern California, as waves of layoffs hit the defense industry. A slump on Wall Street in the early 1990s triggered a glut of For Sale signs in and around New York City. And energy-dependent states such as Colorado and Texas, which had never really recovered from the mid-1980s decline in energy prices, had their woes compounded by the credit crunch of the early 1990s. At one point, NCNB (now part of NationsBank), a bank that was in the thick of the S&L cleanup in Texas, became known among wags as "No Cash for Nobody."

Most real estate markets have now recovered substantially from their slump of the late 1980s and early 1990s. But it left deep financial scars among many baby boomers and essentially destroyed the myth of real estate as a solid investment among both boomers and their newly chastened parents. The drop in real estate prices was a signal event because it taught millions of Americans the downside risk of using leverage— that is, large mortgage debt—to finance real estate investment.

During the bull market in real estate, leverage was wonderful. Using leverage, a down payment of $15,000 could be coupled with a loan of $135,000 to let a homeowner buy a property worth $150,000. If that property doubled in value in a few years, which was not uncommon in the 1970s and 1980s, the house could be sold for $300,000. That meant a profit of $150,000 on an initial investment of $15,000—a ten-to-one payoff. Certainly, real estate brokerage commissions and a few years of mortgage payments should be figured into such calculations, but those were chump change compared to the huge capital gains. As Archimedes said, "Give me a lever and I can move the world."

What many failed to realize until the real estate bear market in the early 1990s was that leverage works in reverse as well. When housing prices fell by 30 percent in many markets in the early 1990s and layoffs forced many to sell their homes in weak markets, the arithmetic became extremely painful. If the $150,000 house had to be sold for $105,000, or a 30 percent loss, not only was the homeowner's equity—the $15,000 down payment—wiped out, the homeowner was also "upside down" in the mortgage, obligated to come up with another $30,000 to pay off the balance of the $135,000 loan. And real estate commissions and monthly mortgage payments were no longer chump change for workers who had been laid off and had their home equity wiped out. Call it Archimedes's revenge.

For many boomers who ended up in such a bind, bankruptcy was the only option. Not surprisingly, personal bankruptcy rates soared in the early 1990s, with 900,000 consumers declaring insolvency in 1992, a postwar record. In contrast, during the entire decade of the 1950s, there were only 584,000 bankruptcy filings. Ominously, despite an impressive economic recovery in the mid-1990s, consumer bankruptcy filings hit a new record of 1.12 million in 1996, and credit card debt has soared. While recent tax law changes may have contributed to the surge in bankruptcy filings, many baby boomers are apparently using credit card debt aggressively to try to maintain their standard of living.

Many economists and politicians were genuinely surprised by how much talk of "economic depression" and "national decline" accompanied the recession (and much of the recovery) of the early 1990s. After all, by many measures, the recession was unusually mild and short-lived. But in our opinion, the depth of outcry had much to do with the fall in real estate prices. The slump not only hit people in their pocketbooks, it also hit hard psychologically by undermining the entire foundation of the American dream: get a job, buy a house, and live happily ever after.

For many baby boomers, the new lesson was: buy a house, get laid off, and go bankrupt. Certainly there had been layoffs during other recessions in the postwar period. But in many cases, earlier rounds of layoffs represented temporary responses to the business cycle, which were reversed when the economy recovered. More recently, layoffs have come to represent permanent job losses associated with corporate restructuring and downsizing. According to a study by Harvard economist James Medoff, workers between the ages of thirty-five and fifty-four were 55 percent more likely during the 1990s to be unemployed due to permanent layoff or job loss than was true during the 1970s. Likewise, previous falloffs in real estate markets tended to be shorter-lived because of the strong underlying trend in the demand for housing.

HOMESICK

Despite the revival of some real estate markets in the mid-1990s, the long-term outlook for home prices looks fairly grim. Recalling the image of the baby boom as a pig working its way through the body of a python, it's a simple matter of supply and demand. The baby boom generation—76 million strong—has largely passed through its peak home-buying years, with the youngest boomers now thirty-four and the oldest fifty-two. In contrast, the baby bust generation, those now between twenty-two and thirty-three, with only 41 mil-

lion members, is 45 percent smaller than the baby boom cohort.

Barring a massive surge in immigration, the number of
first-time home buyers—generally those from twenty-five to
thirty-four years old—peaked in the late 1980s. A modest
surge in first-time buyers can be expected in the middle of
the next decade, when the echo boomers begin to reach their
late twenties. But that will coincide with an even larger increase in the number of baby boomers reaching their late
fifties, a time of life when many will want to sell their homes
and either downsize or move someplace warm.

Two well-respected economists, N. Gregory Mankiw, of
Harvard University, and David N. Weil, of Brown University,
shocked the real estate industry in 1989 with a careful study
of the economic impact of the age wave on the U.S. housing
markets. Their study predicted that "housing demand will
grow more slowly over the next twenty years than at any time
in our sample [since 1947]. If the historical relation between
demand and prices continues to hold, it appears that the real
price of housing will fall about 3 percent a year. . . . More
formal forecasting . . . implies that real housing prices will fall
a total of 47 percent by the year 2007. Thus, according to this
forecasting equation, the housing boom of the past twenty
years will more than reverse itself in the next twenty. . . .
Even if the fall in housing prices is only one-half what our
equation predicts, it will likely be one of the major economic
events of the next two decades."

The Mankiw-Weil study was well timed because it coin-
cided with a softening of real estate prices in many areas of
the nation at the time, and preceded a sharp decline of prices

in most of the country during the recession of the early 1990s. Home prices rebounded in most parts of the country, along with the economy, by the mid-1990s. But in real terms, adjusting for inflation, prices in many areas have still not recovered to peak levels reached in the 1980s.

Of course, not all economists agree with the dire outlook of the Mankiw–Weil study. One respected researcher in the field, Patric Hendershott of Ohio State University, is more optimistic, arguing that the aging of the baby boomers between now and 2010 will increase both the willingness to pay for housing and the quantity demanded. Both increases will raise real home prices, not lower them. Hendershott's research assumes that housing demand on the part of baby boomers entering their sixties will more than take up any demographic slack in the market because "older households are willing to pay a premium for housing."

We doubt that assumption would pass muster of most real estate agents, who have been deserting the industry in droves. Even as the U.S. economy recovered between 1991 and 1995, the number of realtors in the United States withered by 15 percent, as many real estate companies restructured and scrambled to survive. With growth in the trade-up cohort of buyers—those between thirty-five and forty-four—also likely to slow in coming years, the real carnage in the residential real estate market is likely to come later.

A 1993 study for the U.S. National Institute on Aging essentially confirms the Mankiw–Weil outlook. According to a sophisticated computer model developed by Daniel McFadden, of the University of California at Berkeley, 1980 appears to have been the historical peak for U.S. housing prices, ad-

FIGURE 7. THE COMING COLLAPSE IN U.S. HOME VALUES

U.S. Housing Price Projections

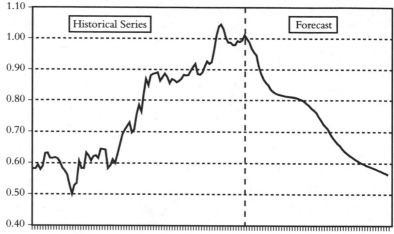

Source: Daniel McFadden, National Bureau of Economic Research

justed for inflation. By 2020, real home prices are expected to have fallen 19 percent from their 1995 level. By 2030, they are expected to have dropped by 30 percent.

A graph generated by McFadden's model is shown in Figure 7. Journalist Craig Karpel, who has written extensively on retirement issues, studied McFadden's research and made the following pointed observations: "The rugged contour of Dr. McFadden's graph, a cross-section of the Matterhorn with the summit already behind us, will be a painful sight for anyone who owns a home. Americans have gotten used to the idea of housing as an investment rather than simply a place to live. But the increase in housing prices was fueled by processes that have totally run their course: the post–World War II economic expansion that produced the baby boom, and the fact that once they were grown up, the baby boomers had to live somewhere. The fantasy that, over the long term, society is going to pay us big bucks to live in our own houses is like expecting not merely to have our cake and eat it too, but to have more of our cake after we eat it. In the economy we're plunging into, a home is going to revert to being what it has traditionally been: a place where you hang your hat—and pay for the privilege of doing so."

Following the slump in housing prices in the early 1990s, it has now become conventional wisdom among baby boomers that one's home will not necessarily be a great investment over the long term. But the myth of real estate investment as a good place to build equity and take advantage of generous tax breaks may take well into the Big Chill period of 2011 and beyond to finally die completely. In other words, while many boomers now understand that real estate may not be a great investment, far fewer are likely to believe that real estate will be a *terrible* investment. Otherwise, there already would be more of a rush to pay down mortgages and to rent rather than buy homes.

If housing prices slide badly again during the next recession, whenever that occurs, housing may finally come to be widely viewed as a terrible investment, which would have enormous consequences for the nation's credit markets and economy. As we consider later, a huge share of the nation's private debt structure is tied up in real estate lending, so a rush to repay mortgage debt could ultimately drive interest rates to shockingly low levels.

If residential real estate markets have already sputtered during the 1990s as the supply of new buyers has shrunk, what will happen when the boomers become active sellers in their sixties? As a recent *Wall Street Journal* article put it: "It's the year 2015. Do you know where your home equity is? For millions of boomers on the verge of retirement, the answer may be gone, vanished, kaput. Thanks to easy lines of home-equity credit, the nest egg may be tapped out. Thanks to a low baby-bust birthrate, there may not be enough growing families to buy the boomers' mini-mansions with three-car garages. And throughout America, boomers who believed too much in the home-appreciation fairy may end up genteelly poor, stuck for the rest of their lives in huge houses that no longer fit their needs."

For the relatively small number of baby boomers who have ample financial assets as a cushion, a slump in home equity would be problematic but not fatal. But for tens of millions of baby boomers, if the Big Chill arrives on schedule in the real estate market, the impact on retirement living standards will be pronounced. As Berkeley's McFadden noted in 1993, "Housing is the most important asset of most elderly households, and for many is the *only* significant asset. . . . [I]n the population aged sixty-five plus, 69 percent of net worth is in house equity . . . and the median equity among holders was $46,192. The only other assets held by a majority of households [over age sixty-five] are bank accounts and equity in automobiles, and the medians among holders of these assets total less than $17,000."

ARE HOMES LESS RISKY THAN STOCKS?

A front-page story in the *New York Times* recently fretted that American households now have 28 percent of their wealth in stocks, with real estate having slipped to second place at 27 percent. Noting that "stock prices are subject to much wider short-term swings than home values," the *Times* article worried that a sharp market decline could "seriously erode the financial well-being of Americans." The implicit assumption appears to be that real estate is somehow a safer asset for households to hold to fund their retirement years than are stocks.

From a demographic perspective, the apparent safety of real estate as an asset class is clearly an illusion. In fact, to the extent that households' investments in real estate have been leveraged investments—that is, based on mortgage borrowings—they are likely to be far riskier in the long run than unleveraged stock holdings. If the Mankiw-Weil or McFadden research is even half right, tens of millions of Americans could see their home equity largely wiped out in what should be their golden years. Compared to that, even a rout in the stock market like those of the 1930s or 1970s may be a preferable outcome for boomer investors.

Essentially, baby boomers are being forced to put an ever-larger portion of their retirement savings into stock because they have no acceptable alternative. Given the low returns available on real estate and cash, arguably the biggest risk boomers face over the next twenty years is not to be invested in equities.

Does this mean that investors should wholeheartedly

trade in their belief in the home-appreciation fairy for an equally naïve belief in the equity-appreciation fairy? Note that even if stocks are "less risky" than real estate in financial market terms, that could mean simply that investors in stocks lose less money than investors in real estate.

Unfortunately, if our nation ignores the looming fiscal crisis associated with the baby boomers' retirement, choosing between stocks and real estate during the Big Chill may be a bit like deciding which of the murderous Menendez brothers you like the most.

5

Stocks and Bonds:
The Long Liquidation

R OCK STAR PETE Townshend of The Who may not have
had his stock portfolio in mind when he wrote the
lyrics "I hope I die before I get old." Now that he has gotten
older, we presume that he's changed his mind about dying
early. We also suspect that he is pretty happy about how his
stock holdings have been doing. If we are right, he should
also be pleasantly surprised about how financial assets perform
during America's Prime Time.

But Pete may eventually return to morbid thoughts about
old age. That's because gains are likely to be hard to come by
during the Big Chill, when all the baby boomers become
natural sellers of stocks, bonds, homes, land, and even collectibles. The whole point of building up nest eggs for retirement is, after all, to sell them when you can no longer work.
If America's Prime Time is when hordes of boomers will be
buying financial assets en masse, the Big Chill is when they
will be selling.

Another Pete, Peter Passell of the *New York Times*, introduced millions of readers to this topic in a rather chilling article in 1996 entitled "The Year Is 2010. Do You Know Where Your Bull Is?" Writing immediately after a sharp dip in the market in 1996, Passell warned of "something far more disturbing two or three decades down the road—when the baby boomers retire and begin to trade in their securities for Winnebagos, visits to the periodontist and trips to Disney World with the grandchildren."

As with the long-run outlook for real estate prices, the stock market issue has been raised quietly by a handful of specialists who study the links between demographics and economics. Once again, their opinions regarding the Big Chill period are, to put it mildly, pessimistic. The experts are, however, decidedly more circumspect about prospects for the equity market than for real estate markets. That partly reflects the dominance among academics of efficient-market theory, which holds that stock markets are essentially unpredictable. Interestingly, that view has been increasingly challenged in recent years by a small group of researchers who have begun to look at demographics as a source of market predictability.

There is also the understandable reluctance of experts to make predictions about the distant future when so many variables, which are themselves unpredictable, can affect the outcome. Bruce Steinberg, chief economist of Merrill Lynch, responded in an understandably impatient manner to the *New York Times* inquiry on the long-term outlook for the market: "Don't bother me with this one—too much can happen between now and then."

THE MARKET MELTDOWN MODEL

Steinberg is right: Looking into the distant financial future is a tough job. Nonetheless, someone has to do it. The work that has been done on the stock market focuses on expected flows of money into—and out of—the nation's employer-based pensions. Other than housing, most personal wealth is accumulated through such pensions, including both "defined benefit" pension plans, which promise a specific monthly pension, and "defined contribution" plans, which are basically tax-sheltered savings plans. Economists John Shoven, of Stanford University, and Sylvester Schieber, of Watson Wyatt, a pension-consulting firm, have conducted careful work on this topic.

Although their research focuses on pension fund flows rather than predictions of the Dow Jones average, Shoven and Schieber's work has clear—and extremely negative—implications for stock and bond markets during the baby boomers' retirement years. In a conversation with the *New York Times*, Mr. Schieber jocularly referred to their key research paper as the "market meltdown paper." Carefully avoiding specific forecasts, Professor Shoven imagined a "1970s-like stagnation in stock prices," which would extinguish many dreams of sailboats and seaside sunsets for elderly boomers.

Shoven and Schieber's work was based on standard demographic projections and a variety of plausible assumptions about the number of workers covered by pension plans, their projected wages, and their life expectancy as retirees. Plugging all these factors into their model, real net inflows into pension plans—contributions and investment earnings, less benefits paid—are expected to rise gradually from $102 billion in 1995 to $149 billion in 2010. Accordingly, the outlook for America's Prime Time is reasonably bullish.

Then comes the Big Chill. By the second decade of the next century, growth in pension assets begins to decline. Adjusted for inflation, the nation's pool of pension assets actually begins to fall in 2025. According to the Shoven–Schieber model, real pension savings will slip from its current level of about 3.6 percent of total wages to zero in 2024 and to −3.5 percent in 2040.

Here's where the numbers become alarming. When hordes of baby boomers cash in, total pension assets are projected to fall to $15 trillion in 2065, from $28 trillion in 2040. In contrast, the total capitalization of listed domestic stocks is currently about $10 trillion. As they say in government, "a trillion here, a trillion there—pretty soon you're talking about real money."

If the real estate markets are any indication, price action can flatten simply when the baby boomers stop buying. In Shoven and Schieber's model, that may not occur until the early 2020s. But financial markets are naturally forward-looking, so prices could falter well ahead of the great liquidation.

Shoven and Schieber were careful to note that they could not predict the size or timing of the impact of pension flows on asset markets with any precision. When pressed, however, Professor Shoven offered a back-of-the-envelope guesstimate of how much stock prices would be depressed. Here he followed a time-honored tradition of economic forecasters (including ourselves): Give them a number or give them a date, but never give them both at the same time.

One way to think about this is to note that each retiree will have to sell his or her accumulated pension

FIGURE 8. WHEN THE BOOMERS CASH OUT

Estimated Net Flow of Assets into or out of Pension and Retirement Savings

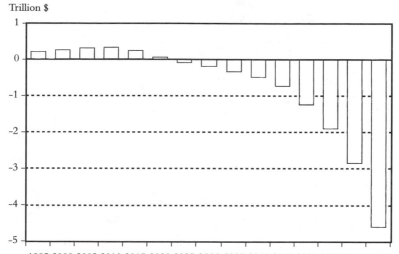

Source: Schieber and Shoven

assets during his or her retirement. But given the demographic trends reviewed above, there will be only
2 workers per retiree versus 3.2 workers today. Thus,
you have only two buyers for the pension assets being
liquidated instead of 3.2 buyers today. Using this
somewhat simplistic logic of a putative shortage of
buyers, asset prices might well fall by up to 45 percent.

Shoven noted that price falls of this magnitude have occurred in almost every generation in memory. But in most
cases, those price falls have occurred due to economic policy
mistakes, such as the failure of the Federal Reserve Bank to
keep the money supply from imploding in the 1930s. According to Shoven, a price decline due to demographics alone

would be unprecedented, comparable in severity to the price drop of the 1970s, but no worse.

One response Shoven received to his back-of-the-envelope forecast was: "Whew, I thought you might predict a debacle like the 1930s." His reply is instructive:

> What they fail to realize is that, if you go decade by decade and take inflation into account, the 1970s were in fact worse than the 1930s for financial markets. Remember that the 1930s witnessed genuine deflation. Real bond returns were not that bad in the 30s. Even real stock returns from January 1, 1930 to January 1, 1940 were better than those of the equivalent decade in the 70s. So the 70s were pretty bad, and represent an upper bound on how bad things might get during the period 2015–2030 when demographics will really kick in.

WILL CASH BE KING?

Another implication of Shoven and Schieber's research is that if the asset price effect occurs, it would likely affect all long-term assets. This means that interest rates would shoot up and depress the value of not only stocks and bonds, but also land, real estate, and even collectibles. The implication is that during this period, the only place for investors to hide would be in short-term U.S. Treasury bills.

To be fair to Shoven and Schieber, as well as to our readers, we would emphasize that they do not advocate that investors head for the hills anytime soon. To the contrary, they expect the asset price effect from demographics to be gradual and to last for decades. In other words, it is not as if every investor will wake up on January 1, 2011, and start selling everything he or she owns because that is the year the boomers begin to retire.

Moreover, even if Shoven's back-of-the-envelope guess is right and stock prices decline by 45 percent during the boomers' retirement years, the level of the market from which the decline begins will make a huge difference to everyone's welfare. In other words, suppose that enlightened economic policies encourage entrepreneurial wealth creation and boost the savings rate over the next decade. Then the Dow Jones average could conceivably rise to 30,000 or higher by the time large numbers of boomers are retiring during the 2010–2020 period. Under such circumstances, there would at least be a reasonably large cushion of wealth in the nation's pension plans and individual retirement accounts to ride out a prolonged bear market.

Siding with every financial planner in the nation, Shoven and Schieber pointed out the disadvantage of having too much cash:

> In the twentieth century the longest stretch of time over which Treasury bills outperformed equities was about fifteen years. We have little else to go on, but we certainly are not advocating that long-term investors invest in short-term instruments to ride out this demographic tidal wave. In fact, it is our opinion that far too many people invest in short-term instruments for long-term accumulations.

We will elaborate on this sound advice when we consider boomernomic investment strategies later.

Michael Hurd, professor of economics at the State University of New York at Stony Brook, is another respected expert on the economics of aging. When asked by journalist Craig Karpel whether the prospect for depreciating asset values is as bad as Shoven and Schieber made it out to be, he was blunt:

> It's probably worse. When the baby boomers are in their sixties, they're going to need to liquidate their individual holdings of stocks, bonds, and mutual funds. The same thing will happen with real estate. Nobody's assets are going to be worth as much. So pension funds will have to sell more of their assets to meet pension obligations than they currently anticipate selling. If anything, Schieber and Shoven's graph understates the problem.

APOCALYPSE LATER?

We side with Hurd in arguing that Shoven and Schieber's scenario for asset price depreciation could understate the problem. Our reasoning is based on Murphy's Law: "If something can go wrong, it will." We would also appeal to O'Toole's Corollary: "Murphy was an optimist."

Our point is this: If demographic forces trigger an asset price decline of 45 percent during the boomers' retirement years, there are likely to be plenty of other problems for financial markets to worry about as well. First, the demographic problem is likely to be international in scope. Both Europe and Japan face even more daunting demographic challenges and, by most measures, are woefully unprepared. So it is conceivable that the international financial system could become dangerously unstable if Shoven and Schieber's "demographic tidal wave" hits all major markets at the same time.

Financial market problems are also likely to trigger political problems as well. As a recent report on population aging from the International Monetary Fund pointed out: "The potentially serious fiscal, economic, and social consequences of population aging raise complex issues, not least of which are political issues that arise whenever the distributional impact of a major public program is reconsidered." Translation: Political interest groups will fight to the death—literally—over who gets the biggest share of a shrinking pension pie. In the United States, for example, ethnic issues could flare up if an increasing number of retired Anglos attempt to impose high taxes on young minority workers to finance their retirements.

Third, if the major industrial economies are thrown into a financial and political quagmire, it will create opportunities for future Saddam Husseins to stir up military trouble with less fear of retaliation. Military experts are already concerned that the graying of America will threaten national security, because there will be a severe shortage of young Americans for the armed forces and limited fiscal resources for military equipment. As some of today's emerging nations, such as China, mature into economic superpowers, the global geopolitical system could shift in unpredictable and potentially dangerous ways.

Fourth, energy shortages could well become a dominant problem during the Big Chill as world oil production tops out. Energy specialists expect conventional oil production to peak sometime during the first two decades of the twenty-first century. Unless alternatives to crude oil quickly prove themselves, "the world could see radical increases in oil prices," according to oil geologists Colin Campbell and Jean Haherrere, writing in the March 1998 issue of *Scientific American*. Moreover, by 2010 the market share of the OPEC states in the Middle East is expected to rise to 50 percent, up from 30 percent at the turn of the century.

Fifth, the age wave is likely to destabilize financial markets not only because there will be more sellers than buyers. Unless major efforts are undertaken soon to rein in Social Security and Medicare programs, the age wave is also likely to contribute to major macroeconomic imbalances as hordes of boomers swamp the system. As we shall see in the next chapter, even if government budget surpluses are the rule during America's Prime Time, massive fiscal deficits could easily return during the Big Chill.

The bottom line: It seems quite unlikely that the only thing investors will have to worry about during the Big Chill is an imbalance of sellers and buyers. Even if Montaigne is wrong about the boomers' souls acquiring a "sour and musty smell" as they age, we conclude that he could be right about their investment portfolios.

Again, we are not trying to scare people into an investment strategy of canned goods and automatic weapons. To the contrary, our scenario for America's Prime Time suggests that the next decade should continue to provide baby boomers with an excellent opportunity—possibly the last in their lifetime—to enjoy solid investment returns and to build retirement nest eggs.

But we do believe that baby boomers need to think seriously about how dramatically the financial climate could change in their retirement years. If that prompts boomers into saving more for retirement, or if it prompts our political leaders into preparing for the age wave, everyone will be better off.

6

Social Insecurity:
The Coming Generational Warfare

THERE IS STILL more than a decade before boomers start to retire in large numbers, but confidence in the nation's Social Security system is slipping badly. The Social Security Advisory Council recently fretted about "unprecedentedly low levels of confidence" in Social Security. In fact, a 1994 survey revealed that more young Americans believe in UFOs than believe they will ever receive a dime in Social Security benefits. Countless articles and news programs about how the financing of Social Security resembles an unsustainable chain letter have undoubtedly sunk in.

We're not sure about UFOs, but we have little doubt that the enormously popular Social Security program will be "fixed" one way or another in coming years. Benefits will be cut, payroll taxes will be raised, and the age for receiving benefits will probably be pushed back toward seventy. A national debate is already under way on how to fix the huge gap in Social Security's long-term finances, and leaders of both political parties are under pressure to come up with a credible solution.

The myth is that Social Security is the third rail of domestic politics—touch this popular program and you're dead. The truth is that politicians of both parties have already performed a line dance on the third rail and gotten away relatively unscathed. This occurred in 1983, when Congress enacted legislation effectively reducing the present value of baby boomers' Social Security benefits by a whopping $1.2 trillion. This was done through relatively stealthy means—the retirement age for most boomers was increased from sixty-five to sixty-seven, benefit levels were cut for those who retired early, and certain benefits were suddenly subject to the taxman's axe.

As economist Laurence Kotlikoff of Boston University points out, the 1983 Social Security changes were worth more than four fifths of all of the debt added to the federal government's books in all of the 1980s. Contrary to popular belief, fiscal policy in the 1980s was not reckless in the sense of placing an enormous additional burden on future generations. That had already been done with huge expansions of so-called entitlement spending programs, such as Social Security and Medicare, in the 1960s and 1970s.

In other words, for all the ink that has been spilled in the media regarding the Reagan deficits of the 1980s, a momentous move in the direction of fiscal conservatism went virtually unnoticed by most commentators. Since most baby boomers in 1983 were then naïfs in their twenties or early thirties, it is not surprising that the gray eminences in Congress were able to cut their future benefits with little outcry.

Now that the boomers themselves are sprouting gray hairs, the debate about their retirement benefits is likely to be somewhat more serious. Led by Boomer-in-Chief Bill Clinton, baby boomers are more politically engaged than they were in the 1980s. Boomer politicians now make up a majority in the House of Representatives. For those interested in preserving the system in its present form—which we are not—the good news is that there is still room for a variety of technical fixes to Social Security: cost-of-living adjustments (COLAs) can be reduced and the retirement age can be tweaked upward. So there is a good chance that such stealth measures to "fix" the Social Security system will be announced in the next few years. At the very minimum, these measures should let the system's actuaries push out the projected date—which is currently 2032—when its combined trust funds go bankrupt.

There is even serious talk of the government investing some of the dubiously named Social Security Trust Fund in the equity market. That has the advantage of letting the actuaries assume higher returns on the trust fund; as almost everyone now knows, the equity-appreciation fairy always delivers higher returns in the long run. While some contrarian investors see that as an ominous sign of a long-term top in the equity market, we see it rather as additional fuel for our scenario for a buoyant market during America's Prime Time. That said, we shudder to think about all the political shenanigans that would eventually flow from making Uncle Sam a large direct shareholder in almost every major American corporation.

Even better, there is growing support for moving in the direction of partly privatizing Social Security. That would let

Americans control some of their Social Security payroll taxes themselves, in private mutual funds, instead of seeing them disappear into the black hole of the Social Security "Trust" Fund. In our opinion, this would be a crucial step in the right direction. Not only would it bring the entire Social Security system under greater public scrutiny, it would also give most boomers a chance for much higher returns.

As we explain later, moving toward a private and fully funded system would look more expensive from a budgetary viewpoint. While that initially sounds like a disadvantage, it would actually expose much that is wrong with the way we account for government programs and act as a check against reckless spending programs.

THE GOOD SHIP *TITANIC*

So, in contrast to our views on housing prices and stock prices during the Big Chill, we're optimistic about how the government will deal with the age wave, right?

Wrong. The problem is that the Social Security system, which is currently the object of so much attention, is merely the tip of the iceberg. According to economists who've studied the numbers carefully, Social Security represents only about 15 percent of the fiscal problems associated with the coming age wave. Fifteen percent is just about how much of an iceberg is visible from above the water.

Not surprisingly, the big money is going to be in rising expenses for health care when the boomers retire. According to the pension-consulting firm Watson Wyatt, "The aging of the baby boom generation will deal a staggering blow to the

U.S. health care system." Everyone who becomes eligible for Social Security on the basis of age eventually becomes eligible for Medicare as well, with Medicare enrollment expected to increase from its current 14 percent of the population to 22 percent in 2030. With costs per enrollee also escalating rapidly, Medicare spending as a percentage of GDP is expected to rise from around 2 percent now to between 7 and 8 percent in the 2030–2050 period.

Despite all the focus on a Social Security fix, potential problems financing Medicare and Medicaid are currently being swept under the rug. So voters must not allow politicians to become too self-congratulatory about dealing with Social Security or running federal budget surpluses in the next few years. Instead they should be asking, *"How will we fix Social Security, Medicare, and Medicaid on a combined basis?"* and, even more important, *"How much will we need to tax our children?"*

Unfortunately, most credible projections of the combined effects of the age wave on America's expensive social programs show the good ship *America* steaming toward an iceberg. As on the good ship *Titanic*, the decision makers on the top deck are currently enjoying wine, women, and song. Lulled into complacency by the good life and smooth sailing, they are not about to be seriously bothered by reports of danger ahead from worrywart technicians.

And the technicians are definitely worried. Consider, for example, a March 1997 report by the Congressional Budget Office (CBO) with the harmless-sounding title "Long-term Budgetary Pressures and Policy Options." Using the gray language of budget bureaucrats, the report recaps the sobering facts of the age wave: fewer workers to support growing numbers of retirees, growing expenditures for Social Security and Medicare, and so on. In other words, the report is based on the same grim arithmetic that drives the Big Chill's scenario for housing prices and stock prices.

The CBO report then plugs in reasonable estimates for how much Social Security and health care expenses will rise as the boomers age, and grinds out various scenarios for the economy over the first half of the next century. These scenarios assume that no major changes are made to the current relatively generous benefit programs. The results are startling.

Virtually every scenario shows a manageable situation during the next decade, when the boomers remain gainfully employed. Responding to recent data showing a better-than-expected budget outcome for 1997, the report notes that "the improved short-term budgetary outlook brightens the long-term picture" and that recent changes "delay any serious trouble for about seven to ten years." That's good, because it supports our own benign scenario for America's Prime Time.

THINKING THE UNTHINKABLE

But here's what the CBO has to say about the Big Chill period, *after* the boomers retire in large numbers:

> Under an array of scenarios with economic feedbacks that assume no change in current budget policy, the debt would increase to historically unprecedented levels in the next four decades. Moreover, as federal debt pushed up interest rates and lowered the growth of the economy, interest payments would begin to

FIGURE 9. SOCIAL INSECURITY

Estimated Social Security and Medicare Income Payments

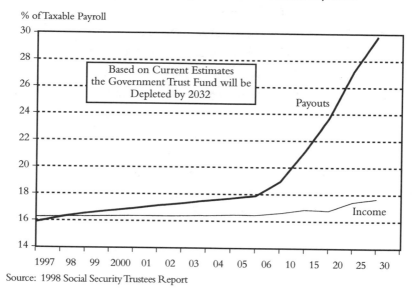

% of Taxable Payroll

Based on Current Estimates the Government Trust Fund will be Depleted by 2032

Payouts

Income

1997 98 99 2000 01 02 03 04 05 06 10 15 20 25 30

Source: 1998 Social Security Trustees Report

consume an ever-larger share of federal spending and eventually grow at an explosive rate. In the end, the total amount of debt held by the public would reach levels that the economy could clearly not support.

Translation: As the boomers swamp the government social safety nets, the budget deficit will explode, bond and stock markets will collapse, and living standards will plummet. It's your basic financial apocalypse.

The graphs that accompany the CBO's report are instructive. As we show in Figure 10, the lines that indicate federal debt as a percent of the economy basically shoot off the charts in the 2030–2040 period. In the CBO's language, such projections support the dry conclusion that "current budget policy is unsustainable, and attempting to preserve it would severely damage the economy."

The lines showing federal debt shooting up to 300 percent of the economy are essentially projections of a potentially catastrophic economic crisis during the boomers' retirement years. Adjusting for the typical timidity of bureaucratic language, this is the equivalent of the CBO's shouting, *"Economic disaster ahead!"* to anyone who will listen. And measured against the scale of the problem, recent efforts to solve the entitlements spending crisis are reminiscent of rearranging the deck chairs on the *Titanic*.

One curious feature of the charts that accompany the CBO analysis is the lines that show projections for real GNP per capita, which is a good indicator of the overall standard of living. Currently, the U.S. economy produces roughly $27,000 in goods and services per person. During the Big Chill period, the CBO graphs show the standard of living beginning to fall and then . . . it disappears! A cryptic footnote explains that "projections of real GNP per capita are truncated when debt held by the public exceeds 300 percent of gross domestic product."

Translation: If debt is allowed to grow as explosively as the CBO's analysis indicates, living standards will rapidly plummet to third-world levels. It's not that the numbers can't be calculated. They are simply too shocking!

To be fair, the CBO emphasizes that such scenarios are not *forecasts* of what will happen to the debt and the economy. Instead, they are just simulations of what would happen if we blindly follow current policies into the twenty-first century.

FIGURE 10. BOOMER DEBT TRAP

Federal Debt (as a percentage of GNP)

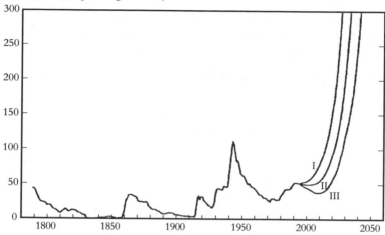

Real GNP per Capita

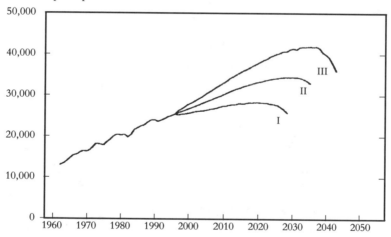

Note: The projections of real GNP per capita are truncated when debt held
by the public exceeds 300 percent of gross national product.

Source: Congressional Budget Office, "Long-term Budgetary Pressures and Policy
Options," 1997.

The implication is that there will be no choice other than to make painful adjustments.

As the CBO points out: "Policymakers would certainly take the necessary steps to limit the growth of debt before it reached unthinkable levels. But because debt can quickly snowball out of control, policymakers would need to act well before it reached a critical level."

So we all can rest assured. Adjustments will be made. Steps will be taken. Whew!

DOOM-O-GRAPHICS

That leaves a few minor questions to tackle: How big will the "adjustments" have to be? Who will actually take the "necessary steps"? And how long can we wait before debt reaches a "critical level"?

The first question is the easiest to answer. The necessary adjustments are huge. Moreover, because of the laws of compound interest, the longer we wait to make them, the larger and more painful they will be.

Alan Auerbach, of the University of California at Berkeley, has spent the last several decades thinking about such issues. As one of the nation's leading experts on fiscal policy, he estimated in 1997 that the size of the permanent cut in government spending (or increase in taxes) needed to stabilize America's finances is roughly 5 percent of GDP, or about $375 billion.

Let's put that figure into perspective. Consider that in a garden-variety economic recession, real GDP might fall by 2 percent. That degree of disturbance to the economy typically generates enormous economic pain and dislocation, alarmist media commentary, and huge political problems for the incumbent president. George Bush was hounded out of office to a large extent because he presided over a 2 percent peak-to-trough economic contraction ahead of the 1992 election.

What politician is going to be brave enough to voluntarily lead the charge to cut spending or raise taxes by a whopping 5 percent of GDP? That amounts to roughly 25 percent of all federal government spending! Imagine all the programs that would have to be eliminated and the huge permanent layoffs of federal government employees that would be implied. If you don't want cutbacks in programs, imagine personal tax rates rising to nearly 60 percent or corporate tax rates to 50 percent.

The first inclination of all politicians confronted with numbers this big is to let others deal with the problem later. Politicians' time horizons are unlikely to stretch much beyond the next election. Naturally, almost all will be inclined to wait and see what needs to be done once the boomers start to retire.

Professor Auerbach estimated that if politicians wait until the year 2017 to deal with the problem, the cost will rise to a permanent cut in spending (or hike in net taxes) of 7 percent of GDP. In other words, if we wait, another 2 percent of GDP per year in permanent "adjustments" will be required to avoid moving toward an American debt explosion worthy of a banana republic.

Why does the bill rise so much if we wait? The basic issue is this: How can the nation build up a collective nest egg for the boomers' retirement years? Just as is the case for any individual, if you start saving early, you can put aside a modest amount every year and let the power of compound interest work in your favor over many years. If you wait until you are fifty-five to save for retirement, you will have to tighten your belt far more aggressively because there are fewer years remaining to build the nest egg.

Suppose we do "fix" Social Security and keep the budget balanced over the next several years, as currently seems possible. Auerbach's work still points to the need for another fiscal tummy tuck of close to 3 percent of GDP—that is, another painful recession's worth—right now, or we face a much bigger bill in the future.

LEAVE IT TO BEAVIS

Now that we've established how big government funding problems are likely to be during the Big Chill, let's think about who will end up bearing most of the costs.

Economist Laurence Kotlikoff of Boston University has developed a type of analysis called "generational accounting" that estimates how much of the burden for government spending is likely to be borne by each successive generation. Using basically the same type of chilling data that leads to uncontrollable debt explosions in the CBO analysis discussed above, he calculated in 1994 that, under then-current policy, future generations would face an 82 percent lifetime net tax rate!

This reminds us of Groucho Marx in *A Night at the Opera*. After inviting a wealthy society matron to dinner, he was confronted with a large bill that he could not afford. Rising angrily, he handed the bill to the matron, declaring, "This is ridiculous! If I were you, I wouldn't pay it!" He then stomped quickly out of the restaurant.

Kotlikoff's work is another clever way of showing that U.S. fiscal policy is on an unsustainable path. For boomers, it suggests a simple choice: Cope with some combination of higher taxes and lower future benefits beginning soon, or face draconian choices after retiring. For younger generations, it suggests that they face an acceleration of what is now a century-long process of making each successive generation pay more taxes than it receives back in benefits.

Naturally, Kotlikoff's 82 percent net tax rate on future generations will not materialize. That's because our political system is basically designed to produce compromises. If it's a question of cutting retirees' benefits or raising taxes on existing workers, we can expect a little bit of both. If it's a question of whether to tax the wealthy, the middle class, or the poor, the answer is all of the above. If it's a question of making painful choices now or letting our children deal with the problems, we will try to spread the pain.

Of course, the political system is hardly unbiased. As noted earlier, middle-aged and elderly voters tend to have a disproportionate voice in policy decisions because they vote with much greater frequency than the young. So as the baby boomers age, gray power will become an increasingly formidable force at the polls. As aging boomers fight harder to prevent their benefits from being cut, the bills will fall on their children and their children's children.

In short, our political system has a Leave-it-to-Beavis bias that will try to saddle Generation X and younger cohorts with the ballooning costs of caring for the boomers in their retirement years. Accordingly, many analysts have warned of coming generational warfare during the Big Chill period, when painful fiscal adjustments will finally become unavoidable.

Our best guess is that over the next decade the political system will deal with about one third to one half of the entitlements spending problem. Many of those cuts will come through relatively painless measures that will reduce boomers' future entitlements before they are fully aware of what they are losing. Such cuts represent the low-hanging fruit available to politicians who are serious about the crisis.

But this scenario still leaves massive adjustments of 3 to 4 percent of GDP that will urgently need to be tackled during the boomers' retirement years. Such adjustments are likely to be far more painful and politically contentious. By then, all of the low-hanging fruit will have been picked, and politicians will need to propose highly controversial cuts in medical benefits for boomers, or onerous tax hikes for their working children and grandchildren.

Journalist Craig Karpel writes imaginatively of formerly affluent yuppies "picking through dumpsters for cans to sell and scraps to eat." He envisions this group ending up as "dumpies": Destitute Unprepared Mature People. Such scenarios are probably too extreme, because we have seen other modern industrial economies successfully make massive fiscal adjustments of the size needed in the United States. The recent examples of Italy and Sweden come to mind. Their fiscal cutbacks have been extremely painful, but hardly apocalyptic.

That said, the politics of such adjustments are almost certain to be extremely contentious. It is highly predictable that as the boomers age, U.S. politics will become more polarized. Boomer politicians who dedicate themselves to preserving generous entitlements for seniors with inadequate savings should find large audiences. Likewise, young politicians are likely to prosper if they specialize in fending off tax hikes required to fund retired boomers. Fed chairman Alan Greenspan recently warned Congress about the political consequences of failing to address Social Security and Medicare finances. Such consequences, he warns, "are going to be terribly destabilizing to this society, because you're going to force a wrench between the younger people in our society at that time and those who are in the process of retiring."

WILL WEALTHY BOOMERS ESCAPE TO CYBERSPACE?

If generational warfare breaks out between elderly boomer politicians and Young Turks, both groups may find one common target to bear the burden of tax hikes and benefit cuts: wealthy retired boomers. When the boomers are retired, there will be relatively fewer taxpayers, so politicians will be tempted to move gradually from the taxation of labor income to the taxation of capital income or of wealth itself. Their motivation will be similar to that of Willie Sutton, who, when asked why he robbed banks, replied, "Because that's where the money is."

Benefit cuts for wealthy boomers can be arranged easily through so-called means testing. If you saved for retirement and have assets, presto—your benefits are reduced. Likewise, future politicians will eagerly eye increased taxes on interest, dividends, capital gains, and corporate profits, which will be key sources of income for retired boomers. Owners of luxury homes or second homes will be tempting targets for special real estate taxes as municipalities respond to a relative dearth of taxes from income. As the first wave of boomers begins to die in large numbers, politicians can be expected to push for higher estate taxes to help pay for the remaining boomers—and to take advantage of the large number of estates changing hands.

Aesop's fable of the ant and the grasshopper will be highly relevant to retired boomers: Those who have diligently scrimped and saved for the long winter could end up penalized by having to pay for free riders—those who could have saved earlier but didn't. As Social Security experts Eugene Steuerle and Jon Bakija have pointed out: "Suppose taxpayers A, B, and C have equal lifetime incomes, but only A and B save for retirement, and B gives his savings to his children. Taxpayer A is rewarded for her prudent behavior by being forced to transfer money to both B and C. This is patently unfair. Efficiency violations are severe also. By saving more, the taxpayer decreases the transfer she will receive at retirement; by working more, she pays more taxes to support others but not to provide for her own retirement."

We expect the demand for tax avoidance strategies to soar among wealthy retired boomers during the Big Chill period. But their legal options will be quite limited, since they will be targets of revenue-hungry politicians representing much larger numbers of young people and financially strapped boomers. That means any remaining loopholes in existing tax laws are likely to be tightened at the same time that new taxes on wealth and capital income are raised.

We would also not be surprised to see offshore tax avoidance proliferate during the Big Chill, legal or not. This would most likely be aided by computer encryption technologies. Unbreakable digital codes would permit retired boomers to escape to cyberspace to manage offshore assets with no digital trail for inquisitive IRS agents to follow.

Aware of this risk, the U.S. government is currently trying to regulate the sale of strong encryption technologies. However, its efforts are being opposed vigorously by American business interests, who argue that strong encryption will be vital if Internet commerce is to flourish. This issue bears close watching, since the easy availability of offshore tax avoidance strategies could become a major constraint on government spending throughout the industrialized world in the twenty-first century. A tax system that becomes both onerous and unenforceable as the boomers age would face the real risk of collapse.

ETHNIC AND IMMIGRATION FACTORS

The nation's shifting ethnic mix is likely to be another key political factor during the boomers' retirement years. Whites' share of the population is expected to decline from roughly 75 percent in 1990 to barely more than 50 percent in 2050. That reflects the fact that minority groups have both younger populations and significantly higher birthrates than whites. According to sociologist Steve Murdock, by 2050 "the population will be one in which an increasing number of elderly Anglos may be dependent on young minority populations."

Warming up for the coming political battles, an Internet

page by Raoul Lowery Contreras recently held forth on the topic of "The Future Enslavement of My Hispanic Cousins by an Aging White America." Commenting on a report by the Social Security Advisory Council, Mr. Contreras asks, "Will the booming Hispanic, mostly Mexican-origin, population of America be enslaved by Baby Boomer Social Security checks in coming years?" Now confined to the fringes, such rhetoric could become commonplace during the Big Chill.

Immigration is also likely to become an important political issue during the Big Chill period. One potential solution to the coming shortage of young workers would be to liberalize immigration policy. That would permit foreign workers to come in as the baby boomers retire and the labor force contracts. But it would also require a major shift in U.S. immigration policy and invite an influx of immigrants that would rival the immigration waves that took place in the late nineteenth and early twentieth centuries.

In short, not only do retired boomers face the prospect of generational warfare, which brings their interests into conflict with those of the young, they also face the prospect of intragenerational warfare, which will pit boomer against boomer, depending on how much they have saved for retirement. Now add declining financial markets and potentially divisive ethnic politics and immigration issues to this mix. The result will be huge pressure on the nation's political system during the Big Chill period. It remains to be seen whether such pressure will trigger a major political earthquake or merely set off frequent tremors.

Part III

How to Prosper During the Coming Age Wave

We can work it out.
—*THE BEATLES*

PART I OF this book described a benign scenario for the next decade, called America's Prime Time. If we are on target, it suggests that the great bull market in financial assets that began in the early 1980s will have staying power through much of the next decade. That means there will still be extraordinary opportunities for baby boomer investors to make money and create ample nest eggs for retirement.

Part II described a grim scenario called the Big Chill. If that scenario is correct, there will be a sea change in the financial environment as large numbers of boomers begin to retire and liquidate financial assets en masse. Just at the time baby boomers will need their nest eggs the most, it may become extraordinarily easy for investors to lose money in all asset markets—stocks, bonds, and real estate.

For investors, these scenarios are likely to trigger two basic emotions: greed and fear. If the America's Prime Time scenario is correct, the stock market could conceivably triple—or even quadruple—over the next ten years. Many analysts on Wall Street were shocked when the market hit 9,000. Imagine the shock if the number hits 35,000. If you have even a bit of greed in your bones, you may want to understand why that could happen and how you should best be positioned.

Anyone who tells you they really know what the next few decades will bring is either dishonest or foolish. We have based our scenarios on what we think is fairly reliable research and on our own hunches, which have served us well in the past. But let us emphasize one thing: These are only scenarios, akin to well-informed science fiction. They have also been presented as polar extremes, to give you some sense of the wide range of potential outcomes that the future may bring. If you want to know a dirty secret that many Wall Street gurus and academic pundits never share, repeat the following mantra several times until enlightenment comes: *No-bah-dee-noze.*

We have deliberately played on your emotions of greed and fear, because these are the two strongest emotions that affect your behavior as an investor. If you make investment decisions, you will undoubtedly encounter these emotions and will need to cope with them successfully. And almost all of us have to make, or help make, important investment decisions. These include obvious investment decisions like choosing what kind of mutual funds to own in your retirement savings plan. But choosing your career and helping your children choose their careers are also important investment decisions. Career decisions involve spending large amounts of your most precious commodity of all: your time on this planet.

If Part I triggered emotions of greed and Part II triggered fear, Part III is about how to control those emotions using common sense. Common sense starts with recognizing that we don't really know what the future will bring, so it makes sense for most of us to diversify our investments to protect ourselves—and to benefit from—a wide range of possible outcomes. That's what asset allocation is all about. In the next chapter, we discuss how boomernomic thinking might be applied to the most important type of investment decision— where to keep your money.

Even if we diversify our financial investments, most of us have to make at least one very narrowly targeted investment: our career. Or we may wish to tilt our stock investments or mutual funds toward certain industries whose long-term prospects look especially promising. That's where we believe boomernomic thinking can help out. In Chapter 8 we point out which careers and industries should do well, or do poorly, as the huge boomer generation ages. These conclusions provide no guarantee of quick riches, but it can't hurt to invest with the demographic odds in your favor.

After scaring many of our readers—and ourselves—with some grim facts and academic forecasts about the Big Chill period, we feel obliged to share some good news. To be sure, the economic challenges of the age wave look daunting. However, we believe these challenges also present huge opportunities for America. For example, according to Harvard economist Martin Feldstein, moving to a privatized Social Security system could raise the well-being of future generations by an amount equal to 5 percent of GDP, and raise the nation's wealth by $10 trillion to $20 trillion. Comparable improvements in the nation's standard of living are possible if we make greater use of market principles in our health care system.

These are obviously controversial proposals, but let the debate be joined now, when there's still plenty of time to avoid the Big Chill. In the last chapter we discuss what we call the Big Fix, which focuses on these proposals along with some other ways to rethink the concept of retirement as the boomers enter old age. To be sure, boomers will slow down as they age. But, on average, they should enjoy longer and healthier lives than any other generation in history. In our opinion, senior citizens who wish to work beyond age sixty-five should not be forced prematurely into early retirement. After all, there is likely to be a shortage of workers—and taxpayers—as the boomers age, and we need to retool our thinking accordingly.

The Chinese character for "crisis" is built from two characters, one meaning "danger" and one meaning "opportunity." The Big Chill represents the potential economic danger implied by the aging crisis. The Big Fix is about the major opportunities we have for rethinking our fundamental assumptions about how to provide for older citizens effectively and compassionately.

7

Boomernomic Investing: How to Catch the Age Wave (Without Wiping Out)

I F YOU TAKE our scenarios literally, you may be thinking that our investment advice is to:

- Sell your home immediately and move your family into a studio apartment.
- Borrow every penny you can and invest it in the stock market until 2010.
- Load the boat with health care, technology, and financial services stocks that will benefit from coming demographic trends.
- Plan to cash out all your investments in 2010 and hunker down for the coming bad years.

Actually, these are *not* our recommendations. Our first piece of advice is: Please do not take our scenarios literally. We are the first to admit that our scenarios could be wrong and that there are many other factors beyond demographics that should be taken into account in making investment decisions. We will discuss some of those factors in this chapter, but we emphasize that this book is not intended as an introductory course on investing or personal financial planning. There are plenty of good books available on those topics (see Appendix 1 for references).

Our second piece of advice is: If you have major investment decisions to make, you would probably benefit from professional advice. You can get such advice from a qualified financial planner or an experienced and well-trained stockbroker (also known as "financial consultants") from a major brokerage firm. This is especially true if you are confused or impatient in thinking about our scenarios, or if you are a victim of "analysis paralysis" when dealing with your finances. Financial professionals are paid to think about such issues every day, and to manage their clients' expectations and emotions in making decisions.

As with other professionals, like accountants, doctors, and plumbers, financial professionals' services will not be free. Likewise, it is worth your time to check references and inquire about their training and professional qualifications when your hard-earned money is at stake. There may also be an advantage in dealing with professionals from large, established firms. That's because large firms tend to have the best training programs and the most at stake in protecting their reputation by demanding high standards for their employees' professional conduct.

Many people who wouldn't dream of mowing their own lawn or painting their house are reluctant to pay for financial planning advice. It may be that they are afraid to admit to their own ignorance in such an important area, even though they have plenty of company. Or, to the contrary, they may have read enough to understand the basic principles, which are in fact pretty simple, but never get around to implementing a disciplined financial plan. We are bullish on the financial services industry for the next decade for a simple reason: Tens of millions of baby boomers are now reaching a stage of life when they need professional help in investing but don't have the time or inclination to do it themselves.

GREAT EXPECTATIONS

Our third piece of advice is: Have an open mind about what the future may bring. Use demographic insights to tilt the odds in your favor—not to make wild bets. Many investors are understandably nervous about the stock market because it's done so well in recent years and because valuation measures, such as the price-earnings ratio, look quite stretched by most historical yardsticks. Others may indeed have unrealistically high expectations, as indicated by a 1997 survey of 750 mutual fund investors by Montgomery Asset Management. That survey showed that investors expect average annual returns of 34 percent over the next decade, far better than returns achieved by legendary investor Warren Buffett over the course of his career.

Somewhere in the middle, between paralyzing fear and irrational exuberance, lies common sense. That should include an appreciation that being out of the stock market completely carries its own risks. "Do what you will, the capital is at hazard," wrote Justice Samuel Putnam in 1830 when he developed the foundation for what has come to be known as the "prudent man rule," which dictates how trustees are expected to invest funds for others. As trustee to yourself or your family, you could do worse than follow Justice Putnam's advice to "observe how men of prudence, discretion, and intelligence manage their own affairs, not in regard to speculation, but in regard to permanent disposition of their funds, considering the probable income, as well as the probable safety of the capital to be invested."

This means recognizing that there is no way of avoiding risk of one type or another with your hard-earned money. Hide it under a mattress or hold it all in "safe" bank accounts, and you are exposed to erosion of its value by inflation and lost opportunities for better gains if the stock and bond markets do well. Invest your capital in the stock and bond markets, and you may have to deal with the stomach-churning volatility of market prices.

What may be most unsettling about today's financial environment for most baby boomers is tied to the mixed messages they are hearing from the financial community. On one hand, most boomers are having it drummed into their heads that they need to save more and that stocks are the best place to be for the long run. On the other hand, they are hearing reasonable warnings from luminaries such as Federal Reserve chairman Alan Greenspan about "irrational exuberance" and the need to dampen their expectations. What's a boomer to do?

Even though our scenario for America's Prime Time may play right into the recent extreme optimism of many investors, it can also be viewed as a contrarian scenario. That's because it goes against the grain of many experts' opinions on the stock market, which have generally been cautious in recent years.

WHY THE EXPERTS ARE CAUTIOUS
ON THE STOCK MARKET

Those of us who subscribe to business publications often find our mailboxes stuffed with promotional literature from investment newsletters warning of the great financial crash just around the corner. Such newsletters—and most Wall Street strategists—do not have a good track record in calling the twists and turns of the market.

That said, their warnings are not always completely unfounded. Many simply appeal to the well-known financial principle of "reversion to the mean," which is a somewhat more precise version of the idea that the good news has simply gone on for too long. Historically, periods of above-average market performance have often been followed by periods of below-average performance. The basic idea is that the market tends to be riskiest when stock prices have been high. And measured against corporate earnings or dividend payouts, stock prices have been high.

Joining the newsletter writers, Federal Reserve chairman Alan Greenspan has warned that some investors' enthusiasm may not be well grounded. Likewise, an in-depth research report prepared by John Cochrane for the Federal Reserve Bank of Chicago in 1997 analyzed the unusually high returns from stocks in recent years and warned not only of "reversion to the mean" but also that the high average returns of the last fifty years are themselves difficult to rationalize.

Whenever you hear a Wall Street analyst on television confidently asserting that some stock is overvalued or undervalued, they always have some concept of "reverting to the mean" in the back of their mind. The question is, which mean? One widely used measure of the stock market's valuation level is the so-called dividend yield on stocks. That measures how much annual income investors can expect to receive from owning a share of stock, measured as a percent of the stock's current share price.

Using the dividend yield as a measure of fair value, the U.S. stock market has been wildly overvalued for most of the decade. At the end of 1997, for example, the dividend yield on the broad market, as measured by the Standard & Poor's 500 index, was a paltry 1.6 percent, versus a forty-year average of 3.5 percent. To restore the historical relationship, corporations would have to boost their dividends immediately by 2.2 times, or stock prices would have to fall by nearly 55 percent. An only slightly less extreme conclusion holds if one looks at the market's price-earnings ratio, which was 23.5 at the end of 1997, compared to a forty-year average of 14.6.

Financial economists who've studied whether the dividend yield is a useful indicator of the market's future potential returns have concluded that it has little predictive power for a one-year forecast. But for looking ahead five years, the dividend yield appears to explain something like 60 percent of the variation in stock returns. Picking up on such a relationship, John C. Bogle, founder of the Vanguard Group of mutual funds, noted that "at the close of 1992, with the yield on stocks well below 3.5 percent, historical experience suggests that there is no more than one chance in 16 that stocks will achieve an annual return of more than 10 percent in the next decade."

As discouraging as these statistics are, they are also potentially misleading in a major way. All such statistics really do is verify that stock valuations were low in the 1950s, before the bull market of the 1960s; that valuations were high in the mid-1960s, before the bear market of the 1970s; and that low valuations in the 1970s preceded the current boom. Basically, there are only three real data points, which is not much to hang a theory on. Research by the Chicago Fed, which pointed this out, observed honestly that "with more sophisticated tests, return predictability actually has about a 10 percent probability value before one starts to worry about fishing and selection biases." Translation: *No-bah-dee-noze.*

Such complete honesty about how little we can glean about the future from past data is refreshing. Not surprisingly, such honesty is unlikely to earn you a place as a confident talking head on financial news shows.

We are perhaps more skeptical than most analysts about reversion-to-the-mean thinking for three reasons. First, we are aware of its weak statistical foundation, as just noted. Second, we saw close up how easily stock valuations in Japan broke completely free of their historical moorings. Third, and most important, we see powerful demographic and economic forces ahead that conceivably could keep U.S. market valuations in uncharted territory for an extended period.

"THIS TIME IT'S DIFFERENT"

Seasoned market players point out that markets are often most vulnerable when analysts rationalize high prices with arguments such as "This time it's different." So it is with some trepidation that we argue that current demographic trends are unprecedented. The number of boomers is huge relative to the preceding generation, and they have now reached a stage of life when they are natural buyers of stocks. At the same time, the more conservative political climate has fostered the lowest inflation and interest rates in decades, as have the forces of technology and globalization.

Suppose, for whatever reason, you believe that inflation and interest rates are likely to head back up toward levels of the 1970s or 1980s. Then, yes, stocks should be hit hard and the reversion-to-the-mean view would be correct. If renewed inflation provides investors with another chance to get double-digit returns from government bonds or money market funds, then stock prices would have to fall sharply in order to make the yield on stocks more competitive.

But what if inflation stays low over the next decade and bond yields decline further? Under that scenario, which we think is quite plausible, stocks should continue to post impressive gains. The key is whether interest rates can return close to levels last seen in the 1950s and 1960s, as inflation already has. Consider that consumer price inflation in the United States was only 1.7 percent in 1997. That was below the average level of 2 percent that prevailed in the ten years from 1956 to 1965.

For historical perspective, recall that in the late 1950s the yield on ten-year U.S. government debt averaged only 3.5 percent, as shown in Figure 11. Three-month U.S. Treasury bill rates averaged only 2.6 percent, and consumer price inflation averaged 1.7 percent. If inflation remains low in coming years, we would not be surprised to see interest rates declining substantially, even if they do not return all the way back to the levels of the late 1950s.

FIGURE 11. BACK TO THE 1950s?

	CPI Inflation (%)	Discount Rate (%)	3-Month T-Bill (%)	10-Year Treasury Note (%)
1955–1959 Average	1.7	2.5	2.5	3.5
1960–1965 Average	1.3	3.4	3.1	4.1

Source: Economic Report of the President

BUYING PANIC AHEAD IN GOVERNMENT BONDS?

If baby boomers decide to step up their savings rate in coming years, there could well be a buying panic with respect to government bonds. That's because the government itself, concerned about the Social Security and Medicare funding issues we've discussed, is currently planning to run fiscal surpluses for the next decade totaling more than $600 billion. This means that just as the boomers come into their peak saving years, the government will be creating a scarcity of bonds by buying back its own debt. The likely result: higher bond prices and lower interest rates.

Naturally, if a recession comes along, government borrowing would rise and $100 billion deficits could easily reemerge. But at the same time, a recession could trigger higher savings by households by creating another downdraft in real estate prices. As we discussed earlier, it makes no sense for homeowners to make large interest payments on depreciating assets. If housing prices slide again, large numbers of baby boomers can be expected to accelerate their efforts to pay off their mortgages, which would require higher savings.

Overall debt growth in the 1990s has been anemic by historical standards. Given our cautious outlook for housing over the next decade, we see little risk of an acceleration of demand for mortgage debt. If anything, it would not be surprising to see debt growth slow further if pressure persists to keep government spending in check. Under these circumstances, the main force that would keep interest rates from returning to the levels of the late 1950s or early 1960s would be fear of rising government deficits later, when the boomers retire. If the government took meaningful steps to deal with the entitlements spending problem, bond yields could plummet further. But don't hold your breath.

JAPAN'S MARKET MANIA: CAN SOMETHING SIMILAR HAPPEN HERE?

As we have observed in Japan, the sensitivity of equity market valuations to declining interest rates can be extraordinary. Recently, even amid poor expectations for profit growth, the Japanese market has sustained a price-earnings ratio of more than 40 since the yield on government debt has been less than 1.5 percent.

Using a garden-variety model of equity valuations, we posed several simple "what if" scenarios. For example, what if earnings growth over the next decade slows from the double-digit rate of recent years to a more moderate but healthy pace of 7 percent? That would imply a near doubling of corporate profits by 2008, which would not be out of line with historical experience. Then suppose the yield on ten-year government bonds falls to 4.5 percent, or a full percentage point higher than where it was in the late 1950s. Under that scenario, fair value for the S&P 500 index would be 3,000, compared to a level of 970 at the end of 1997.

In other words, under that scenario the level of the stock market would more than triple over the next decade, with the price-earnings ratio on the market rising to 31.5 from 23.5 at the end of 1997. Using the more popular Dow Jones stock index, that would equate to a rise in the Dow from 7,908 at the end of 1997 to 27,000 by 2008. Since that sounds like a quote on the Tokyo stock index in the late 1980s, you may understand why our experience with Japan has affected, if not distorted, our perspective.

And it gets wilder. If U.S. government bond yields were to fall to 4.0 percent by 2008, with the same assumptions as above, fair value for the S&P 500 could be as high as 4,500, which would imply a price-earnings ratio of 47 or an equivalent Dow Jones average of 37,000. Basically, the more serious the government gets in "fixing" Social Security and Medicare, the more room for interest rates to drop, and the more room for baby boomers to build wealth for retirement.

Not surprisingly, if earnings growth slows to 4 or 5 percent and bond yields rise over the next decade, the market would likely post unimpressive gains. But conventional models of stock valuations tend to be highly sensitive to the yield on U.S. government bonds. Even under assumptions of slow earnings growth of 4 to 5 percent per year, a drop in long-term interest rates to 4 percent would result in a tripling of the market over ten years. No wonder Bill Clinton's political strategist James Carville wanted to be reincarnated as the bond market.

Please note what we are *not* saying. First, we are not trying to predict where the Dow Jones average will be next year or the year after. Only clairvoyants can do that. We are also not ruling out the possibility of a sharp correction in the market over the next few years. That could come about from an overheating economy, from an interruption to foreign capital flows or other external shocks, or even from economic problems that some fear will be triggered by the year 2000 computer problem.

What we are saying is that conditions are ripe for equity valuations to break free from their historical moorings if inflation, interest rates, and fiscal policy continue to follow recent trends. In fact, the parallel to Japan is notable in another respect: Japan's drop in bond yields in the 1980s was in large measure a product of the government's desire to fix its own fiscal mess, which was created in the 1970s, when large deficits were in vogue. By squeezing the government's budget in the 1980s, Japan's policy makers set the stage for bond yields to drop and equity values to soar.

BOTTOM LINE FOR BOOMERS: "JUST SIGH AND JOIN THE PARADE"

What if we are completely wrong and it turns out that a massive bear market is just around the corner? For boomers who are saving for retirement—that is, with a thirty-year horizon on a good fraction of their money—the historical data have a clear message: Stick with stocks, but don't get addicted to recent double-digit rates of return. According to Jeremy Siegel, of the University of Pennsylvania's Wharton School, the real returns to stocks have far outpaced the returns to bonds or cash on a thirty-year horizon for virtually every period he has studied. For example, stock investments made at the peak of every major market cycle this century have recovered their real value and, on average, quintupled in real terms over the subsequent thirty years. In other words, even hapless investors who bought stocks in August 1929 or January 1966 would have seen healthy returns if they held on to their investments.

Other academics have some nits to pick with such analysis. Most important is that the number of real data points is still small; major bull market peaks have occurred only in 1901, 1906, 1915, 1929, 1937, and 1966. And the United States was lucky enough to avoid major calamities that resulted in complete wipeouts or closure of other equity markets in this century. Moreover, going back 150 years, Siegel did find one thirty-year period when both bonds and cash outperformed stocks. That was the 1831–1861 period, when the approaching Civil War was not well received by the financial markets. Boomers' faith in the long-term case for stocks implicitly assumes that an approaching generational war will be less disruptive to the markets.

As John Cochrane's research for the Chicago Fed wryly observed, perhaps the U.S. market's impressive returns over the last century are "the opposite of the old joke on Soviet agriculture—100 years of good luck." Now that everyone has figured out what a good investment stocks have been, the nation has built huge institutions that allow wide participation in the market. "If so," Cochrane concluded, "future returns are likely to be much lower, but there is not much one can do about it but sigh and join the parade."

If our scenario for America's Prime Time is correct, tens of millions of boomers will have no choice but to sigh and join the retirement savings parade. If the government cooperates with policies that keep inflation and interest rates low, the parade may continue to be reasonably enjoyable. On the outside chance that the government gets serious about addressing the entitlements spending problems, the stock market would likely shoot the moon. In any event, serious sighs should probably wait for the Big Chill.

Confused by what to do? Our advice is to follow the KISS principle: Keep It Simple, Stupid. Despite the risks outlined above, young savers with many years to go before retirement should probably stick to an asset allocation of 70 to 80 percent in equities and 20 to 30 percent in bonds, with minimal holdings of cash (that is, bank deposits or money market funds). Middle-aged boomers with a moderate risk tolerance should probably stick to an equity position of 55 to 65 percent of their overall portfolio, with the remainder in bonds and perhaps 5 to 10 percent cash. For elderly investors, or those with little tolerance for risk, an equity position of 40 to 50 percent may make sense, with as much as 20 to 25 percent of the remainder in cash.

Rest assured, there is no scientific way to determine the best asset allocation for an individual. One old rule of thumb that seems as good as any is that the bond portion of your portfolio should be roughly equivalent to your age. The remainder would then be in equities. For example, if you are forty years old, you would have 40 percent in bonds and 60 percent in equities, unless special circumstances dictated a more cautious or aggressive position. The more cautious the investor, the larger the share of bonds or cash.

If you are concerned that the markets have succumbed to irrational exuberance, there is a clear implication: Save even more than you have been saving, on the basis of expected lower returns. The other reason that most baby boomers should consider saving more is that surveys show many boomers are saving only about 30 percent of what they need even without taking the rate of return issue into consideration.

Economist Shoven advises investors to be prepared for real rates of return over the next few decades that are in the 4 to 5 percent range instead of the double digits they have become addicted to. Even though we are somewhat more bullish than Shoven about the next decade, his outlook makes perfect sense in thinking about average returns over the next several decades. Unless we have suddenly become a nation of Warren Buffetts, no one should count on persistent returns of 30 percent plus.

If our scenarios for America's Prime Time and the Big Chill are even roughly on target, the implication would be to stay reasonably aggressive for the next decade and then move to a somewhat more conservative position as the eldest boomers approach retirement age. Think of it this way: In recent decades it has typically been a winning strategy to figure out what the front-end boomers were investing in, and go along for the ride. When they were investing in real estate in the 1970s and early 1980s, it was a good time for anyone to invest in real estate. When they turned to stocks in the 1980s, it was a great time to do the same. If they move more into bonds as they age, don't be surprised to see bonds outperform stocks for unusually long periods. And tilt your asset allocation accordingly.

Legendary mutual fund manager Peter Lynch once said, "Gentlemen who prefer bonds don't know what they're missing." The last century of statistics backs him up. But he wasn't investing during the Big Chill. If we are correct, the old investment rules may be less than helpful during the Big Chill, when return *of* capital may become more important than return *on* capital. Bonds are likely to play a larger role in front-end boomers' portfolios as they age. When the majority of the boomers are actually elderly, it could be that cash is king. So bonds and cash should probably play a larger role in your portfolio as the boomers advance in age. That reflects the basic rule of boomernomic investing: Get there before the boomers.

NEW RULES FOR REAL ESTATE

As noted above, we emphatically do not recommend selling your house because of our demographic prognostications. Transaction costs are too high to move based on a long-term demographic projection, and you have to live somewhere, anyway. In addition, your local market undoubtedly has its own dynamics that need to be considered. And even if you believe our long-run outlook for real estate, your spouse may think we are lunatics. Better to keep the peace at home.

But if you have to move, or are thinking about moving anyway, you may wish to readjust your thinking about real estate. In our opinion, housing should be thought of mainly as a fundamental lifestyle decision, not a surefire investment. Rules of thumb that worked for boomers' parents, such as "Always buy the biggest house you can afford" or "Put as little in your down payment as possible," could easily be a trap for younger Americans. If we are correct, it may pay for boomers to be relatively conservative about housing (1) by sticking to homes they can easily afford and (2) by paying off the mortgage ahead of schedule. The new rule of thumb is likely to be "Don't borrow against a depreciating asset." For boomers, borrowing against real estate should be thought of in the same terms as borrowing to buy a car: a necessary evil, not a get-rich strategy.

Not everyone will agree with the last point, since keeping a big mortgage may provide boomers with extra capital, which can then be put in the stock market and earn high returns. That puts the miracle of leverage back to work for investors, with the added kicker of a tax deduction for interest payments on the mortgage loan. In effect, much of the American public has adopted that strategy in recent years, since many have accumulated sizable stock or mutual fund portfolios before paying off their mortgage. If our scenario for America's Prime Time is correct, that strategy may continue to work brilliantly. But we have one observation: It's very risky. Just ask millions of Japanese homeowners who took on big mortgages in the late 1980s, when they felt wealthy because of their inflated stock holdings. They then had to contend with declining stock prices and home prices in the 1990s and still feel the pain.

As Canadian financial consultant and demographic pundit David Cork argues, "Real estate is turning into a stock market. On any given day, some stocks go up and some go down. In real estate, we are seeing the same thing." We concur. We also believe that the three major drivers of real estate will continue to be location, location, location. The outlook for home prices is likely to depend critically on local factors, which in some cases may well be capable of bucking the demographic forces we discussed for the Big Chill.

Just as there are always some attractive stocks during a bear market, there will be some local markets and regions that may do well even as the age wave hits the overall real estate market. Likewise, certain types of homes may be better suited for aging boomers than others. For example, ranch homes or other single-story homes will probably hold their value better than sprawling three-story Victorians as the boomers age. The reason: fewer stairs to climb. Likewise, attractive town homes in good locations may do well as more boomers reach the empty-nester stage of life and wish to avoid the hassles of home maintenance.

Over the next decade, the biggest demographic play in real estate is likely to be in retirement property and second homes. Most Americans are reluctant to purchase a vacation home until they are over fifty. As increasing numbers of boomers reach the half-century mark, the demand for this kind of housing is likely to grow strongly. The type of properties that could experience the greatest price appreciation will be those that satisfy the dual needs of boomers who are looking for a vacation getaway as well as a place to reside during retirement. This suggests that resort areas that are within a two-to-three-hour drive of a major city should do well.

Surveys by real estate agents suggest that roughly one quarter of all second-home owners plan to turn their vacation residences into retirement homes. If anything, we would expect this share to rise in coming years as more boomers seek out dream locations for retiring. And as boomers move into the age bracket between fifty-five and sixty-four, real estate agents say, they are far more likely to own a second home.

Based on boomer demographics, vacation properties in prime areas are likely to be solid investments—at least over the next decade. The most desirable properties will naturally be those in sunny climates near a beach, a lake, or the mountains. Accordingly, we anticipate that some of the hottest real estate markets in coming years are likely to be places like Vail, Colorado; Sante Fe, New Mexico; Phoenix, Arizona; Naples, Florida; and Taos, New Mexico. The sleeper of real estate markets could be oceanfront properties in Oregon, a low-cost state known for its tough stand on environmental issues.

Even though demographic trends look highly favorable for the market for second homes, don't expect a repeat of the real estate mania of the 1970s or 1980s. The reason is that second homes are a luxury, not a necessity. Only 7 percent of adult households purchase second homes, and second-home buyers can afford to be choosy about how much to pay. After all, they already have a place to live.

Another caveat is to consider not only the likelihood of increasing demand for second homes, but prospects for increasing supply as well. Builders may well flood the market with retirement condominiums in Florida in coming years, which will keep prices down. Second homes with unique properties, like a lakefront or oceanfront setting, should do better than those located "near" a golf course. There is plenty of room in Florida to build new golf courses, while there is a limited supply of oceanfront property.

Finally, if we are right about wage trends—that is, the rich getting richer—luxury second homes are likely to do better than middle or low-end properties. At least that should be the case until the local wealth police—also known as the condo cops—start slapping huge property taxes on luxury properties during the Big Chill.

8

Boomernomic Wave Watching: What Industries Will Prosper?

IF THE BASIC rule of boomernomic investing is to get there before the baby boomers, demographic insights should be helpful in predicting which industries will prosper and which will not. Like today's global positioning systems that assist automobile drivers in getting to a desired location, demographics can lead investors to attractive places at the right time. As Foot and Stoffman note, when you live in a country where almost one third of the population is reaching the same stage of life over the same twenty-year period, then you own an investment road map drawn on a large scale. This map should be helpful in career planning for you and your children, and for tilting your (properly diversified!) investments so that the demographic odds are in your favor.

Getting ahead of the boomers over the next decade means anticipating what products and services the front-end boomers will need. As a wave watcher on the lookout for emerging trends, the key is to watch what today's adults in their early fifties are doing. A convenient place to start is with the Boomer-in-Chief himself, Bill Clinton. For example, when press stories circulated last year about President Clinton getting fitted for a hearing aid, we made a mental note to check into the hearing aid industry, which should benefit from the millions of boomers who will be needing hearing aids in coming years. As we noted from the articles on President Clinton, boomers' demand for hearing aids is likely to be particularly strong because of the damage done to their eardrums from years of attending high-decibel rock concerts. Likewise, the eyeglass industry has been taking off in recent years and should continue to prosper as more boomers turn forty. Why? For the simple reason that 80 percent of people over forty need eyeglasses.

Based on the fact that ten thousand boomers per day are plunging into their fifties, what are tomorrow's other boomer-based growth industries? Here's a list of our favorites: preventive health care, travel, leisure and entertainment, financial services, and technology.

BIONIC BOOMERS

From a long-term perspective, health care will undoubtedly be the industry most affected by the age wave. Imagine what the United States will look like in the year 2050, let alone the rest of the developed world. The share of the U.S. population age sixty-five or older will have nearly doubled to 21 percent from 12.5 percent today. The number of people age eighty-five or older will have grown to 19 million from 3 million in the 1990s. By the year 2050, some 42 percent of sixty-five-year-olds will survive to age ninety, up from only 7 percent in 1940 and 25 percent today. This may turn out to be a conservative projection. Advances in the life sciences that we discussed in Part I could push the life expectancy of retirees even higher. On current trends, the first half of the twenty-first century looks set to become the age of the bionic boomers.

The sheer number of aging Americans is likely to cause an explosive increase in the demand for health care and long-term care. The share of the population in nursing homes is expected to double over the next fifty years. At the same time, the fraction of the population with disabilities is expected to rise by nearly two thirds, with annual hospital stays per capita projected to rise by about one third. With boomers' bodies wearing out just as the government is trying to keep a lid on health care costs, private firms that help deliver health care in a cost-effective manner should be in hot demand.

Just as school construction surged when the boomers reached school age, the demand for health care facilities should eventually soar as baby boomers move into their fifties and sixties in large numbers. Older boomers will be less likely to relocate to a community that lacks a top-notch hospital. Hospitals that are viewed as a financial burden in the mid-1990s will be an important economic development tool for some small cities and rural districts after the turn of the century. After 2010, many small communities will also be the sites of new retirement communities to house the World War II generation and the early boomers.

Remember, during the next decade the boomers will be

getting older but will not be elderly. Their bodies will be starting to wear out after half a century of eating rich foods and watching TV. Health care problems in the next decade are likely to focus on deteriorating vision, creaky bones, clogged arteries, enlarged prostates, impotence, and the advent of menopause. Drugs and medical devices that can help deal with the health problems of middle age—especially without surgery—should be in big demand.

The surge in medical and nursing care expenses associated with old age is still fifteen to twenty-five years in the future. During their fifties the boomers are likely to focus on preventive medicine, better nutrition, and home fitness equipment. Industries dedicated to meeting these needs should prosper in the next decade.

ALL ABOARD

The travel, leisure, and entertainment industries are also likely to witness explosive demand growth in coming years. As with real estate, certain segments of these industries will be affected much more than others. We believe the travel and travel-related industries are among the biggest beneficiaries of the age wave. Cruise lines and airlines are likely to be the preferred modes of transportation of boomers to destinations around the world. The demand for luxury travel tours should also surge, since people over the age of fifty-five purchase roughly 80 percent of the luxury travel in America.

Meanwhile, leisure is the dominant national pastime for men and women over sixty. Golf and golf-related industries should benefit for at least the next ten years from the aging of the largest golfer population group in history. Boomers play golf more than any previous generation. Even billionaire boomer Bill Gates has gotten into the swing, as evidenced by his recent television endorsement of Callaway golf clubs. As the boomers march on toward retirement, they will spend an increasing amount of time on golf courses around the nation. Some analysts expect total spending on golf to reach nearly $30 billion by the year 2005, up from $16 billion in 1994.

Entertainment will also continue to be a growth industry in the years ahead. However, the kinds of entertainment the boomers spend their money on will undergo a transformation. As boomers' children grow up, boomers will have more time to putter around their homes or just indulge themselves. That suggests rising interest among boomers in cooking, gardening, home improvement, and other low-key, home-oriented activities. Industries that should be able to profit from this aspect of the age wave include those related to books, furnishings, and gardening.

As Foot and Stoffman point out, "Gardening is the classic case of an activity that the 20-year-old has no time for and the 50-year-old loves. Gardening is an excellent business because gardeners need a constant supply of things: bulbs and seeds and fertilizers and tools and books. Someone is going to do such a good job of supplying these things that her operation will become the Body Shop of the gardening business."

Aging boomers who are not homebodies may well be spending more time at casinos. Gambling is currently one of the fastest-growing leisure activities in North America for a simple reason: Gamblers tend to be people in their fifties and sixties who have spare time and spare money. As more boomers move into this age bracket, the gambling industry should continue to prosper.

FINANCIAL NIRVANA?

If our outlook for America's Prime Time is even half right, the next decade should continue to be a prosperous one for the nation's mutual fund companies, brokerages, insurers, and financial planners. As we have discussed, the fastest-growing portion of the population over the next decade will be people age forty-five to sixty. That group is becoming increasingly obsessed with retirement at a time when Washington is likely to be drawing in the safety net.

But a mid-1990s Merrill Lynch study showed that boomers are saving barely a third of the amount they need to make it comfortably through their retirement years. In addition, the boomers have been forced to become investors as companies increasingly push employees toward "defined contribution" pension plans such as 401(k) plans. Those plans force employees to make many investment decisions themselves, resulting in huge growth in the number of people who need investment advice.

Likewise, boomers are entering their peak saving years at a time when many are expected to receive large windfalls in the form of inheritance. According to a study by Cornell professors Robert Avery and Michael Rendall, the boomers are expected to inherit $10.4 trillion in the next decade. That money will be up for grabs, along with other boomer assets; many people in this age bracket have already forsaken traditional bank accounts for mutual funds and other financial vehicles such as variable annuities.

FIGURE 12. SAVERS ON THE RISE

U.S. Spenders and Savers (Share of Total Population)

Percent

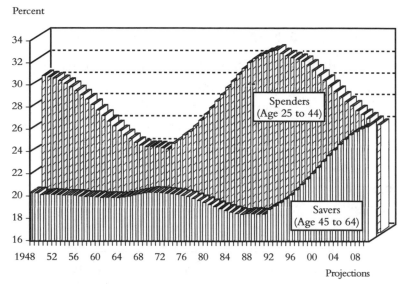

Projections

Source: U.S. Census Bureau, WEFA

In the last few decades firms in the financial services industries that cater to large institutional investors have prospered as the pension industry boomed. Although institutional pension assets should continue to grow, as we discussed earlier, firms that serve the needs of individual investors should be especially well positioned as the boomers age. Typical customers of mutual funds, stockbrokers, or financial planners are people in their fifties or sixties who have extra money to invest. At the same time, such customers are likely to be pressed for time and mature enough to recognize that they need advice. As the number of fifty- and sixty-year-olds surges in the next decade, the financial services firms that prosper will be those who persuade their customers to "leave the driving to us."

Perhaps this demographic backdrop explains Nobel laureate William Sharpe's decision to launch a company called Financial Engines, which will provide investment advice to retail investors over the Internet for about $25 per year. Professor Sharpe, who was a pioneer of modern financial theory, plans to offer small investors the kind of rigorous portfolio consulting that in the past has been available only to large institutional and corporate investors for huge fees. This does not mean that you will need a Nobel Prize in economics to be a financial planner in coming years. But it does suggest that financial planners will need to offer a high level of personal service to compete with what will be available cheaply thanks to modern communications tools.

SUBSTITUTING CAPITAL FOR LABOR: THE CASE FOR TECHNOLOGY

The final sector we are highlighting as a major beneficiary of baby boomer demographics is technology, especially firms that produce hardware and software for the information processing and communications industries. We are talking about a boom in capital spending, not consumer gadgets. (Gadget buying will come from the echo boomers, who are entering their teen years in large numbers.)

There are several reasons to expect an extended, demographically driven boom in capital spending. Labor force growth is projected to slow down markedly in coming years, implying an increasing scarcity of labor. For example, over the 1994–2005 period, the labor force is expected to increase only 14 percent, compared to a rise of 24 percent in the preceding decade. And the slowdown in labor force growth will become more pronounced as the boomers retire in large numbers.

This slowdown should help real wages begin to rise again after a long period of sluggish growth while the boomers crowded the labor market. That should prompt firms to invest heavily in laborsaving equipment and technologies, especially if such technologies are falling in price while wages are rising. Given the dramatic cost declines we are seeing in the computing and telecommunications industries, firms should have every incentive to continue to invest heavily in coming years. Taking into account increased competition from low-wage nations overseas, the case for substituting capital for labor is even more compelling for U.S. firms.

If America actually begins to save more as the boomers age, interest rates should decline, lowering the cost of capital even further. This ties in with our view that price-earnings ratios will rise to unprecedented levels during the next decade, providing the nation's entrepreneurs with an extraordinary opportunity to raise capital and fund new businesses.

As technology investor Michael Gianturco points out in a book called *The Market That Beats the Market*: "When Microsoft's Chairman, Bill Gates, became the wealthiest man on the *Forbes* 400 list for the first time, in 1992, there should have been an audible bang. Gates's accession to the top spot on our list made a clear and absolute statement about technology in America, to wit: what we used to think of as the technology sector of the economy—a sort of curious, arcane, and spe-

FIGURE 13. SUPER SENIORS SOAR

U.S. Population 85 Years and Over

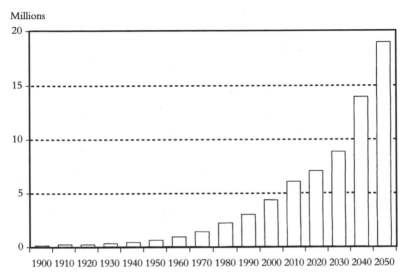

Source: U.S. Census Bureau

cialized business off to one side, a nerd business—had *become* the economy."

If that was true in 1992, it is true in spades now. Since 1992 Bill Gates's net worth has risen from $7 billion to somewhere close to $50 billion and Microsoft has become the second-largest stock in America's stock market, as measured by total market capitalization. There is obviously much more going on here than demographics, as we discussed in detail in Chapter 2. That said, if we are correct about a demographically driven rise in savings and wages, those forces will continue to promote the rapid emergence of a technology-driven "New Economy" over the next decade.

OTHER DEMOGRAPHIC FACTORS

We have focused on demographic trends related directly to the boomers, but such an approach to investing must also consider some of the other major trends that will be driven by demographics in coming years. As shown in Figure 14, the coming bulge in teenage echo boomers is the second most important demographic factor that should affect the U.S. economy over the next decade. With the ranks of teenagers expected to swell by nearly 5 million, the industries that seem best positioned to benefit are entertainment, casual apparel, and consumer electronics.

Less obvious, but of potential importance to investors, is the rapid growth of those older than seventy-five. While their numbers are currently relatively small compared to the boomers, the oldest of the elderly are the fastest-growing part of the population. According to the U.S. Census Bureau projections, the population age eighty-five and over will more than double during the next twenty or so years, from three million to seven million. By the year 2040 this age group will again double in size, to fourteen million. By 2050 the oldest old would be nearly 5 percent of the total population, compared to just over 1 percent in 1994. The obvious beneficiaries of this trend are nursing-care companies and providers of medical diagnostic services and equipment.

THE QUALITY IMPERATIVE

As baby boomers age they are likely to place increasing importance on quality and service and less importance on price.

FIGURE 14. PROJECTED U.S. POPULATION CHANGE
1995–2005

Millions

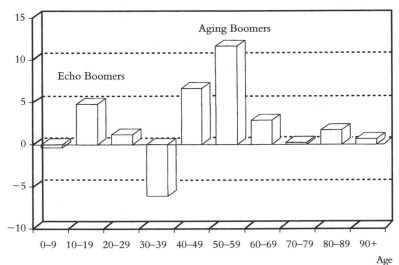

Source: U.S. Census Bureau

This is a trend that will cut across industries and have great importance to anyone marketing to the boomers.

As Canadian demographic experts Foot and Stoffman note, young people tend to have little money and lots of time. They therefore tend to have plenty of time for bargain shopping and checking out lots of stores before making a purchase. If they buy a stereo or a computer, they may not mind spending a lot of time putting it together, as long as the price is good.

In contrast, middle-aged people tend to have more money but less time. They are likely to have more responsibility at work and at home and less time for do-it-yourself projects. They are not as likely to shop around for bargains and are more willing to pay premium prices for quality products that work as they are supposed to. They are more likely to pay others to deliver or assemble goods because their time is valuable.

If there is any truth to these stereotypes, it holds major implications for retailers and other businesses that are marketing to the boomers. Companies like Wal-Mart, Home Depot, and Price Club, which emphasize cheap prices, may have been ideally suited to the needs of young, price-sensitive boomers. Clearly, these retailers' strategies have to change as the boomers become more service- and quality-oriented.

Foot and Stoffman believe the glory days of large retail shopping malls are over because middle-aged boomers' tastes are shifting. Instead, they predict a revival of Main Street as older, affluent consumers decide to shop at neighborhood bakeries, butcher shops, or clothing boutiques where the staff knows customers' likes and dislikes. If they are correct, it would point to an improvement in urban life after several decades in which malls and megastores dominated the market.

SOME CAVEATS FOR WAVE WATCHERS

If we are right about which industries will prosper as the age wave progresses, those industries should probably offer more opportunities for both employees and investors than other sectors. As usual, however, there are a few caveats that should be kept in mind.

The first caveat in thinking about any market is to consider both demand and supply. Yes, the demand for financial services is likely to be excellent over the next decade, but there is already a glut of capacity in the financial markets. That's why megamergers in the banking and brokerage industries are occurring. So even though the industry may do well overall, there may be great turbulence *within* the industry as it tries to cope with excess capacity.

The second caveat is to consider the mounting financial pressures on governments. Yes, the demand for health care will rise in coming years, but the government will be under great pressure to reduce its expenditures in that area. So the sector is likely to grow, but pressures for cost cutting and consolidation will be intense. Firms that can provide cost-effective delivery of services are likely to prosper, but other firms will be squeezed as cost pressures mount. Investors in the sector and prospective employees will need to be very careful about how specific companies are positioned to cope with the coming cost squeeze.

The third caveat is that boomernomic career thinking should be applied quite differently to someone who is forty-five compared to someone in his or her early twenties. For the forty-five-year-old, being a financial consultant might be a great career for the next decade. But a new college graduate might want to think twice about getting into the financial services industry. That's because the industry's demographics are likely to deteriorate sharply just when today's graduate should be in his or her peak earning years. If the Big Chill scenario is even half right, then someone should write a song called "Mama, Don't Let Your Babies Grow Up to Be Stockbrokers."

The fourth caveat for investors is never to confuse a good

company or a good sector with a good investment. A great company that has a high valuation could well turn out to be a disappointing investment, especially if any negative news surfaces about the company or the sector. Conversely, a lackluster company that has a low stock price can turn out to be a good investment, especially if positive news comes out. Accordingly, we would never blindly recommend that investors put their money into a few stocks or sectors just because the demographics are favorable. In our judgment, good investing always involves (1) broad diversification and (2) a careful evaluation of growth prospects—which can be greatly affected by demographics—against how much one has to pay in the market for growth.

A CORE-AND-SATELLITE APPROACH
TO FUND INVESTING

Most investors are well served by letting a mutual fund manager make stock selection decisions. Few people really have the time to do their own homework on stocks. Take our recommendation with a grain of salt, because we are in the mutual fund business ourselves, but funds are growing because they offer people a convenient way to invest while letting others—whose careers are on the line—do the legwork.

Our recommended approach to investors who want to profit from the age wave is to take a core-and-satellite approach to mutual fund investing. We would start with the conventional recommendation that investors keep the bulk of their stock investments, perhaps 70 to 80 percent, in broadly diversified portfolios. For core positions, most financial advisers might recommend funds that measure their performance against the S&P 500 index. We part company with some advisers by recommending a core position in global funds that include foreign market exposure. The performance of global funds is measured against broad global indexes such as the Morgan Stanley Capital International World Index or the *Financial Times* World Index. Global funds have not performed as well as U.S. funds in recent years, so American investors are now understandably skeptical about investing outside the United States. That said, the U.S. market has become quite expensive relative to foreign markets, so this is probably the best time in years for American investors to consider international diversification.

The satellite funds around the core might include four or five specialty funds, which target sectors with favorable long-term prospects. The specialty funds are likely to be far more volatile than the core funds. When they do well they should do very well, but when they fall, they will fall harder. Accordingly, each of the satellite funds should represent no more than 5 percent or so of one's overall stock market exposure. That way, one can live with the considerable volatility that might prompt an investor to dump a fund just at the wrong time, passing up the opportunity for strong gains over the long haul.

Based on boomernomic thinking, we would focus on health care, financial services, technology, telecommunications, and emerging markets. With this kind of fund structure, an investor can have a broadly diversified portfolio, but with a few modest tilts toward sectors that appear to have favorable long-term prospects.

The core-and-satellite approach reflects an old saying in the investment world: "If you want to get rich, concentrate; if you want to stay rich, diversify." The core funds should be broadly diversified and no riskier than the overall market. In contrast, the satellite funds permit the investor to make a few concentrated bets in high-octane sectors with the hope of getting exceptional returns. If those hopes are frustrated, the core funds should act as a cushion.

Even the best investment plans may eventually be for naught if the government fails to address its looming fiscal crisis. As we noted earlier, one should probably expect them to take a flurry of half measures. What we would really like to see is the Big Fix, which would give people far more control over—and responsibility for—their financial future. What's at stake is nothing less than the future success of the American economy—and thus the world's.

9

The Big Fix: What the Government Should Do

IN ANCIENT EGYPT the pharaoh was deeply disturbed by his recurring dream of fat calves and withering grain stalks. After his trustworthy analyst Joseph interpreted his dreams as a forecast of seven fat years followed by seven lean years, he took action. By putting aside resources during the fat years, Egypt was able to live through the long drought and prosper once again.

We are disturbed by our bad dream about the Big Chill, as are many other analysts and political leaders who understand demographics and economics. We have no wish to spend our retirement years watching America go through economic and political convulsions that should be avoidable. We are also concerned about the "Brazilification" of our nation's society—that is, the widening gap between rich and poor—and by our strong sense that this trend will accelerate further as the technology revolution and globalization intensify.

With the baby boomer generation now reaching its peak years of earning, political maturity, and perhaps even wisdom, the time to face these issues is now. The good news is that the demographic issues are quite well understood—at least by specialists—and have been debated for years. As a result, there are well-conceived proposals to make greater use of market forces to reform Social Security, Medicare, and Medicaid. These reforms would boost our savings rate, raise the return on retirement assets, and control medical costs in one fell swoop. Quick action in the next few years to privatize the Social Security system and incorporate market principles in our health care system could do much to avoid the looming fiscal disaster that otherwise awaits us during the Big Chill period. Even better, these policies could yield sustained dividends of higher productivity and higher economic growth for baby boomers and their children.

There are also any number of positive steps the government could take to deal with increased economic insecurity and growing inequality associated with the technology revolution and globalization. Some of these are simple and require only that our political leaders understand that many aspects of our current system of unemployment benefits, taxation, and health care were designed for a *Leave It to Beaver* economy of lifetime employment and job stability that no longer exists. Does anyone really believe that health care or pension benefits should not be freely portable from job to job in the high-turnover, rapidly changing environment we have plunged into?

TIME TO RETIRE SOCIAL SECURITY, WITH DIGNITY

America's Social Security system was signed into law on August 14, 1935, and will mark its own sixty-fifth birthday in the year 2000. It has successfully permitted tens of millions of American men and women to retire with dignity after they built the most prosperous nation in history and defended the nation in two world wars. Originally inspired by Otto von Bismarck's pay-as-you-go retirement system in nineteenth-century Prussia, the Social Security system is noble in intent but deeply flawed in design. It is time to retire the Social Security system with dignity, and with ample provisions to grandfather in those who now depend—or are about to depend—on the current system.

Social Security has served its original purpose but has become an increasingly bad deal for baby boomers and their children. In our opinion, it should be replaced with a financially secure, privatized system that will provide better returns on "contributions," as Social Security payroll taxes are disingenuously called.

Even as recently as two or three years ago, those who proposed privatizing Social Security were quickly dismissed as naïve idealists whose only fellow travelers were fringe libertarians. That said, there is now a growing consensus among mainstream politicians that Social Security is in need of radical reform. In response to a public that is clamoring for better options, there is growing support for at least *some* movement toward a privatized system. Likewise, there is also a growing consensus that private capital

FIGURE 15. THE YEAR THE CHICKENS
COME HOME TO ROOST

(Best–Case Estimates of Year Each Trust Fund Will Be Depleted)

Old Age Supplemental Insurance (OASI)	Disability Insurance (DI)	OASDI (Social Security)	Hospital Insurance (HI)
2034	2019	2032	2008

Source: 1998 Annual Report of the Board of Trustees of the Federal Old-Age and Survivors Insurance and Disability Insurance Trust Funds

markets can provide a better return on investment than can government.

With a major debate on the future of Social Security under way, there is now a window of opportunity to reform the system in a way that recognizes tomorrow's demographic realities and takes advantage of what other countries have learned in reforming their systems. In our opinion, moving rapidly toward a fully funded, privatized system offers America its best hope of steering clear of the fiscal iceberg that lurks ahead: an aging population that cannot be supported by the workforce. We urge Americans to support radical reforms to move rapidly to a fully privatized system, and to reject timid half steps or cosmetic measures that will be favored by many politicians.

THE SOCIAL SECURITY DEBATE:
HOW TO DEAL WITH A COLLAPSING
PYRAMID SCHEME

The basic design flaw that now haunts the Social Security system has been explained well by Harvard economist N. Gregory Mankiw. "Social Security masquerades as a pension plan," says Mankiw, "but it's really a pyramid scheme."

The distinction is critical. A pension plan accepts contributions from young workers, then invests them in stocks, bonds, and other assets. It then pays out the return and principal when workers retire. In contrast, a pyramid scheme doesn't really need to do any serious investing. Instead, it offers amazing rates of return to early investors by giving them some of the contributions from later investors. Eventually, of course, the later investors are shortchanged—and are understandably irate. For that reason, pyramid schemes (aside from government-sponsored ones) are now illegal in all fifty states.

According to Mankiw, a person retiring in 1940 earned a phenomenal inflation-adjusted return of about 135 percent on his and his employer's "contributions." Returns like that would make Warren Buffett blush, and were quite popular with the first wave of retirees. Naturally, the trend has been downward ever since. The return was 24 percent per annum for those who retired in 1950, 15 percent in 1960, and 10 percent in 1970. It's down to 4 percent today and is headed south fast. A 1998 study by the Heritage Foundation estimates that a dual-income, thirty-year-old couple with combined earnings of $52,000 can expect a 1.2 percent rate of return. The same study estimates that a single black male, regardless of income, is likely to lose money, receiving 88 cents for every dollar put into the system. Lower returns for black males are based on their shorter life expectancies.

The pyramid is unsustainable. Based on current population trends, the number of people age sixty-five and over will more than double over the next fifty years, but the number of working-age people will increase by only 25 percent. As recently as 1950, there were 16 workers to support every Social Security beneficiary. Now there are only 3.3 workers to support that same beneficiary. By 2025 there will be fewer than 2. Unless society is prepared to tax those poor remaining workers in an extremely punitive fashion, the game is up.

Charles Ponzi, the notorious Boston swindler and pioneer of pyramid schemes, would know what to do: get out of town fast. Unfortunately, the baby boomers as a group do not have that option.

A genuine debate about Social Security has become unavoidable because increasing numbers of boomers and young Americans now understand what a bad deal it is for them. Accordingly, the tide of public opinion is turning sharply in favor of radical reform. For example, in a 1996 public opinion survey by the Cato Institute, 69 percent of Americans favored allowing individuals to opt out of Social Security and invest their payroll taxes in an IRA-type account. Only 12 percent opposed that concept. Likewise, a recent poll for the Democratic National Leadership Council by pollster Mark Penn found that 73 percent of Democrats want the ability to invest all or part of their Social Security taxes privately.

These survey results coincide with indications that most Americans believe Social Security is in trouble and that it won't be there for them. According to another Cato Institute poll, fully 60 percent of all individuals under the age of sixty-five express that belief, as do larger majorities of younger adults.

Essentially, the Social Security debate is about what to do with a collapsing pyramid scheme. While many politicians say they want to save the system, at the same time some are talking about expanding eligibility for Social Security's expensive twin program, Medicare, which is also financed largely as a pyramid scheme. On current projections, the Medicare "Trust" Fund—another accounting gimmick—is scheduled to run dry in 2008, well before the official projection of the depletion of the Social Security Trust Fund in 2032.

A litmus test for politicians who are talking about "fixing" the Social Security system is to ask whether they mean fixing the *combined* programs of Social Security, Medicare, and Medicaid. If the answer is "Let's deal with one program at a time," it is a strong indication that they are not serious about real reform. Likewise, politicians who talk about "strengthening" the system, rather than restructuring or reforming it, can hardly be serious about facing up to the system's true problems. Why should anyone want to "strengthen" a pyramid scheme?

HOW WOULD A PRIVATIZED SOCIAL
SECURITY SYSTEM WORK?

The Cato Institute, in Washington, D.C., has spent years making the case for privatizing Social Security and has worked with some of the nation's most distinguished economists in developing specific proposals. Details are available at Cato's Web site (www.cato.org), along with a useful calculator for projecting how your own retirement income would fare under a privatized system versus the current Social Security system.

The basic idea of a privatized system is simple and can be thought of as a "super IRA" approach. Instead of seeing their Social Security payroll taxes disappear into the black hole of the federal budget, workers would be permitted to put the money into a personal retirement account (PRA) and earn a tax-free market return. As with current IRAs, workers would be able to freely choose which firm they wanted to manage their money.

As with many 401(k) plans, workers would choose from a regulated menu of investment choices, from conservative to aggressive. Likewise, they would receive regular reports (electronically, if they wish) on how well their account was performing. The entire system would come to be managed by private firms in a highly competitive market, and workers would be given periodic opportunities to move their account to a different firm if they wish. In this sense, workers would become valued customers of the private firms that would run the Social Security system. Instead of being captive wards of a faceless government monopoly, workers would benefit from competitive pressures dictating that the customer is king.

The key attraction to workers of a privatized system would be the potential for higher rates of return on their contributions. For example, consider a twenty-two-year-old woman just now entering the workforce with a starting salary of $24,000 and whose wages increase 2 percent per year above inflation. According to Cato's Social Security calculator, she can expect to receive a Social Security benefit of about $19,000 per year (in 1997 dollars), assuming the program is still around in 2042.

If she were permitted to simply place her payroll taxes in a stock fund with a 5 percent real rate of return, she would have a nest egg worth $560,000 in 1997 dollars at retirement age. This would allow her to draw a $50,000 benefit per year until death. This would be more than two and one half times higher than what Social Security offers for the same level of investment, assuming—and this is in all likelihood a faulty assumption—that the existing system's benefit levels won't be reduced even further.

A WORLDWIDE REVOLUTION: WILL AMERICA BE LEFT BEHIND?

One does not have to imagine how a privatized Social Security system would work. There is already a highly successful example of a privatized system that has operated in Chile since May 1, 1981. According to José Piñera, a Harvard-trained economist who designed the system as Chile's minister of labor and social security, the average real return on investment has been 12 percent per year, or more than three times higher than the program's anticipated yield of 4 percent.

In the seventeen years since Chile introduced a privatized system, complemented by other important market reforms, a flood of investment has benefited individuals as well as the economy as a whole. Unemployment has fallen to its lowest level in history, productivity has increased sharply, the savings rate has soared to more than 25 percent of GDP, and economic growth has doubled to a 7 percent average during the last thirteen years.

According to Piñera, the most difficult task was managing the transition to the new system. His team set three simple rules: (1) "Do not hurt your grandmother." That meant guaranteeing benefits to those already retired. (2) "Give workers a free choice." That meant offering the option of staying in the current system or opting out voluntarily. (3) "Do not accumulate more debt for your grandchildren." That meant closing the door to the pay-as-you-go system for young new entrants. They also developed responsible ways of financing the system's sunk costs without increasing tax rates.

Chile's system has proven to be very popular with workers. After workers were given the choice of entering the new system or staying in the old one, one fourth of the eligible workforce chose the new system. Today, 93 percent of Chilean workers are in it.

The Chilean model has already been widely emulated in other Latin American nations and is being studied carefully by countries around the world. China—supposedly a Communist country—has already adopted elements of the system, with workers there now paying half their retirement payments into an individual investment system and half into a traditional social security system. Private social security systems have also been adopted in Great Britain and Australia. As many nations around the world abandon U.S.-style social security in favor of individually owned, privately invested accounts, the United States is being left behind.

As Piñera observed ironically, "When Otto von Bismarck created pay-as-you-go social security in 1883, he never dreamed that most governments in the Western world would adopt his model—and that a century later all those systems would be headed toward bankruptcy. The absurdity of the pay-as-you-go system is comparable to that found in the works of Franz Kafka, whose days working at a social security institution must have been a source of inspiration." Piñera's comment raises an interesting question: How much longer will Washington burden Americans with an archaic, sputtering Social Security system devised for Prussia in the nineteenth century?

BUT ISN'T THE STOCK MARKET TOO RISKY?

Not surprisingly, the biggest objection to privatizing Social Security is, "You just can't trust the stock market." "Why Let Wall Street Gamble with Our Nest Egg?" asked a recent *Business Week* column by Christopher Farrell, who points out that the higher returns of the stock and bond market have historically been accompanied by greater risks. Farrell's suggestions for some "repair work" include trimming benefits by tinkering with Social Security's cost-of-living adjustments. Translation: Further lower the system's rate of return for young Americans. His other suggestion—we're not kidding—is to force into Social Security nearly four million state and local government employees who have opted out of the system. Translation: Find more bodies to force into the tail end of the pyramid scheme. Does anyone care to put that suggestion up to a vote among state and local government employees? With states like Oregon seeking approval to let all of their citizens opt out of Social Security in favor of state-sponsored IRAs, the trend is for greater freedom of choice and worker empowerment, not the reverse. Farrell argues unconvincingly that Social Security is "a compact between generations that would be upset by privatization." What does a compact have to do with a proposal to force in millions who have opted out? This notion of a compact reminds us of Chicago gangster Al Capone's notion of persuasion. "You can get a lot farther with a gun and a kind word," said Al, "than you can with a kind word alone."

Ironically, we suspect that the vast majority of Farrell's financially savvy fellow employees at *Business Week* would be among the first in line to opt out of the current Social Security program and join a new privatized system. Most know that Social Security is an extremely bad investment. With Social Security expected to yield minimal or negative returns for today's young people, one would have to be a very bad investor—or very unlucky indeed—to do worse.

As you may have gathered from our unpleasant scenarios for stocks during the Big Chill period, we are well aware that the stock market is risky—especially if one focuses on year-to-year fluctuations. But what really counts for retirement is the long-term trend of the market over a person's entire working life. Using data going back nearly two hundred years, Wharton professor Jeremy Siegel has documented that there has been no twenty-year period in which the average buy-and-hold investor would have lost money by investing in the U.S. stock market. In fact, there has been no twenty-year period when stocks have fallen behind inflation. Even the worst period during the last century, which included the Great Depression and the 1929 crash, yielded a positive real return of more than 3 percent. The average twenty-year rate of return has been 10.5 percent.

With statistics like that in their favor, no wonder many voters believe that the risk of staying in the Social Security system—which is almost guaranteed to produce poor returns—is higher than the risk of opting out. Even if blind faith in the equity-appreciation fairy is naïve, there may be a reasonable middle ground. Social Security Advisory Council member Sylvester Schieber—author of the "market meltdown paper" we discussed earlier—proposes permitting Americans to divert a large portion of their Social Security payroll tax to IRA-type private accounts. The remainder of the payroll tax would be used to provide a minimum guaranteed benefit to all Social Security recipients.

Schieber's proposal reflects the idea that if a market meltdown were to occur, the government would be on the hook anyway to provide a minimum benefit. Provision of a minimum benefit would return Social Security at least partway back to its origins as a safety net for the disadvantaged. It would place more responsibility on middle- and high-income investors to watch over their own retirement assets—and to assume some market risk. At the same time, it offers them the potential for higher returns in the capital markets and frees them from another major risk—that of having their "contributions" locked into dismal returns through the Social Security pyramid scheme.

BUT WON'T PRIVATIZATION INCREASE THE BUDGET DEFICIT?

Another major objection to privatizing Social Security is that it could increase the government's budget deficit. Suppose workers get to take their Social Security payroll tax and deposit it in their own account. Then the government will lose that tax revenue and the budget deficit will grow again. Isn't that a big problem?

Yes and no. It would certainly be inconvenient for many politicians, who are still congratulating themselves on balancing the budget and who do not want to face up to the baby boomer retirement issue. By pushing up the deficit, it would put pressure on Congress to keep other spending in check and to make government more efficient. In our view, that would be an advantage, not a disadvantage.

As we discussed earlier, there is no room for complacency about America's finances despite the fact that the budget is currently balanced. The budget tells us much more about where we have been than where we are going. Prudent changes to our accounting concepts would clearly show us to be drowning in a sea of red ink. According to former commerce secretary Peter Peterson, "If the federal government accounted for its retirement liabilities the way private companies must account for their pension liabilities, the official annual federal deficit would rise by $800 billion." If Medicare is added in, Peterson estimates the deficit would rise by nearly $1.4 trillion.

When you hear politicians in Washington boasting about the balanced budget, Peterson's assessment provides an important reality check: "If the Social Security and Medicare balance sheets were evaluated according to private-sector accounting standards, both would be declared massively insolvent immediately." According to Peterson, private-sector executives who ran their pension systems this way would be thrown in jail for violating federal pension regulations.

THE NEED FOR
GENERATIONAL ACCOUNTING

There is a better way. Laurence Kotlikoff of Boston University has developed a technique called "generational accounting" that we believe should be part of every regular presentation of the budget outlook prepared by the Congressional Budget Office for Congress. This method of accounting is a comprehensive gauge of all current and future government budgetary policies—and how the benefits and costs of such policies affect each cohort. As such, it gives a more realistic assessment of the burden of government tax and spending policies on past, present, and future generations.

Generational accounting is needed because most budget accounting focuses only on current revenues and expenses of the government. This gives a good picture of where we have been, but not where we are going. Politicians frequently attempt to make budgetary policies more palatable by pushing the tax burden off on future generations. Generational accounting is designed to see through—and prevent—budgetary smoke and mirrors.

The key economic issue of the next few decades will be how to finance the baby boomers' retirement. We badly need analytical tools that are up to the job. Generational accounting would force politicians to regularly report to voters how much of a tax burden we are placing on future generations. Kotlikoff comes up with figures over 80 percent, so his accounting framework has become a political hot potato. In a November 1995 report the Congressional Budget Office concluded that generational accounting should *not* be part of regular budget statements. According to the CBO, generational accounting "lies in the realm of analysis, not accounting" and "depends on uncertain and debatable assumptions."

This is nonsense. If we are to have any hope of dealing rationally with the financial burden of the boomers' retirement, we need more analysis and less misleading accounting. Any budget—including any company's business budget for the current quarter—depends on "uncertain and debatable assumptions." The point of any budget is to make some reasonable assumptions about the future and to make plans based on the best possible information. The political problem with generational accounting is that any reasonable assumptions about the boomers' Social Security and Medicare costs have highly unpleasant implications and cast our current political leadership in a poor light.

If we want our elected officials to get serious about preparing for the age wave, we need to ask them over and over again: "How much are you planning to tax our children?" If they hear this question enough, they will finally be forced to learn the answer—and to start dealing seriously with the issues.

In our opinion, politicians who do not support the regular use of generational accounting in the budget process are not serious about preparing for the boomers' retirement. This may sound like a dry, technical issue—which it is—but regular use of generational accounting would have enormous practical implications for how Washington spends your money.

HEALTH CARE AND MEDICARE REFORM: THE CASE FOR PATIENT POWER

No sector of the American economy is more regulated or more politicized than the health care industry. And no sector is in greater need of radical reform if we want to prepare adequately for the boomers' retirement.

Despite a recent slowdown in the rate of growth of health care costs, attributed to corporate cost cutting and the growth of "managed care," health care spending over the past several decades has been rising at about twice the rate of increase of the gross domestic product. A naïve extrapolation of that trend would suggest that we could be spending our entire GDP on health care by the year 2062!

As we discussed earlier, health care spending is virtually certain to increase sharply when the boomers retire en masse. Not surprisingly, people over the age of sixty-five see doctors nearly twice as frequently as do younger Americans, and enter the hospital twice as frequently. The elderly spend roughly four times per person on health care than younger Americans, and the rate of increase in such spending is nearly three times that for younger Americans.

Medicare and much of our nation's health care financing suffers from the same fatal design flaw as Social Security: It masquerades as a fully funded insurance program but is actually another pyramid scheme. Those who got in early—the boomers' parents and grandparents—have received benefits far in excess of their contributions. That's a major reason why federal spending on each elderly American dwarfs what is spent for each child—by a ratio of ten to one. In contrast, latecomers to the health care pyramid scheme—that is, the boomers and their children—face draconian cost cutting and life-and-death rationing as they age. The recent public backlash against managed care (which rests on bureaucratic rationing) could be just a small taste of what's in store when serious pressure for budget cuts builds during the Big Chill period.

We do not pretend to have all the answers to this complex and emotional issue. As with Social Security, however, our strong sense is that we need to wrest power over this important area of our future away from Kafkaesque health care bureaucracies and put it where it belongs: with consumers. An ambitious set of proposals for how to do this has been laid out in *Patient Power: Solving America's Health Care Crisis*, written in 1992 by health care economists John Goodman and Gerald Musgrave.

The key to patient power is to understand that in a world of limited resources, there are basically only two ways to control costs. One is to let the choices be made by patients themselves. The other is to delegate the choices to health care bureaucrats who ultimately answer to the government. The United States has largely chosen the bureaucratic route, with many politicians fixated on managed care with quasi-religious fervor.

Arguments for enlarging the scope of managed care typically assume that most individuals are not smart enough or knowledgeable enough to make wise decisions. But as Goodman and Musgrave noted, if that argument is persuasive for health care, why isn't it equally persuasive in every other area of life? "With respect to almost any decision we make," argued Goodman and Musgrave, "someone else is always smarter or more knowledgeable than we are. If the case for freedom rested on the assumption that free individuals always make perfect decisions, we would have discarded liberty and democracy long ago."

The case for patient power rests on a different assumption. No one cares more about us than we ourselves do. Prudent people will naturally turn to experts when important decisions need to be made about complex matters, but that is very different from completely turning our lives over to specialists. Americans have become knowledgeable consumers in many complex areas; why not in health care as well?

Health care costs spiraled out of control in recent decades largely because, for most individuals, health care is cheap, not expensive. For example, for every dollar Americans spend on hospital care, on average they pay only 5 cents out of pocket. Likewise, patients pay less than 19 cents out of pocket for every dollar they spend on doctor's services. Accordingly, Americans have generally not felt the need to become knowledgeable consumers of health care. Let the good doctor decide how much to spend, and let the insurance company or government pay the bills.

The fact that we are shielded from the full costs of our health care decisions by the current third-party payment system has created extremely perverse economic incentives. For example, imagine if we only had to pay 5 cents on the dollar for other necessities like food or transportation. Under national food insurance or national transportation programs, demand would soar for gourmet meals and luxury automobiles.

The radical reform needed to solve the nation's health care crisis is simply to apply the same commonsense principles to health care that we do to other goods and services. Goodman and Musgrave propose a system of medical savings accounts (MSAs) to correct the third-party payment problem. MSAs would allow people to save money in tax-exempt accounts, much like IRAs now. Money in those accounts would be used to pay routine medical expenses. So instead of purchasing expensive insurance policies that cover all health care expenditures, people would be able to purchase relatively inexpensive catastrophic-illness insurance policies to protect themselves against major medical bills.

For example, an employer currently pays more than $4,800 to provide health insurance for a typical American couple with two children. With MSAs, the employer could buy a catastrophic-illness policy—with a $3,000 deductible—for about $1,800. They could then pay the worker the $3,000 difference to put in an MSA that could be used to pay for routine medical expenses. Any unspent money would roll over to the next year, with interest.

In a relatively short period of time, most workers would

have a significant pool of money to use in the future. That's because 90 percent of Americans spend less than $3,000 per year on health care. After the balance in an MSA reaches a certain level, workers could transfer the funds to an IRA or 401(k) plan. These savings could also be used for other purposes, such as buying life or disability insurance, making a down payment on a home, or financing education expenses.

Using MSAs, workers would spend their own money for ordinary health care expenses. They would therefore have normal market incentives to control the costs of such care and to seek out doctors and hospitals that provide quality care at a competitive price. That would do much to stimulate true competition among doctors and hospitals to maximize quality and minimize costs.

Goodman and Musgrave estimate that a system combining MSAs with universal catastrophic-illness insurance for the currently uninsured could result in net savings of nearly $170 billion per year, or almost one fourth of what the nation spends on health care. Most of the savings are expected to come from the greater care exercised by consumers about what they purchase, but substantial savings would also come from the reduced need for third parties to generate red tape every time a patient sees a doctor.

Despite heavy discrimination against them in the current income tax code, MSA-type plans have already been adopted in a number of companies, including the Golden Rule Insurance Company, Dominion Resources, *Forbes* magazine, Quaker Oats, and dozens of small businesses. To date, they have been highly effective at controlling costs while preserving quality. They also have been highly popular among workers. Such plans would undoubtedly be even more popular if MSAs received tax breaks to put them on a level playing field with traditional third-party insurance.

As it is, none of the premiums for traditional insurance are taxed as income, but employer contributions to MSAs are treated as regular income. Funds in MSAs are also now subject to triple taxation: the corporate income tax, the capital gains tax, and the individual income tax. That cripples private savings as an alternative to third-party insurance. By enacting federal MSA legislation, Congress could establish a comprehensive cost-control system that would curb costs without bureaucratic rationing.

Another major advantage of enacting federal MSA legislation would be the creation of a system of truly portable medical insurance that would avoid the problem of "job lock" that many workers now face. In the high-turnover world being created by the technology revolution and globalization, workers should be able to use their MSA funds to maintain health coverage while they are between jobs.

Finally, MSAs should eventually become the backbone of the Medicare/Medicaid programs as well. Those programs are becoming unsustainable in their current incarnations. Major cost reductions will come either through draconian rationing—dictated by bureaucrats—or something like MSAs, which create normal market incentives for consumers to control health care costs and to benefit from greater freedom of choice.

A loud and clear message coming from virtually every corner of the world is that free markets work and that socialism, collectivism, and command-and-control bureaucracies do not. That message so far appears to have largely escaped the health care sector, which represents one seventh of the U.S. economy. Without revolutionary change, it is difficult to see how aging boomers will be able to have access to the care they will surely need.

RETHINKING RETIREMENT

When Otto von Bismarck set sixty-five as the magic age for retirement more than a century ago, life expectancy was just forty-five. With modern medical advances, the Social Security eligibility age would have to be raised to something like ninety-five to provide comparable retirement protection today. Even without major new medical breakthroughs, rising life spans are expected to lengthen the period spent in retirement to nearly twenty years by the time the boomers are all retired. And if our read on the biotech revolution is right, medical breakthroughs should be the norm in coming years.

While this is good news to those of us who expect to live to a ripe old age, it is bad news for those who oppose Social Security and Medicare reform. In addition, it suggests that Americans need to rethink the old idea of a rocking-chair retirement beginning at Bismarck's magic age of sixty-five. Many older Americans suggest in surveys that they would like to have some sort of paying job, but few follow through. One reason is because of perverse Social Security and private pension plan incentives that heavily penalize seniors who remain in—or reenter—the workforce. This is a holdover from the 1930s, when jobs were scarce and politicians wanted to prevent older workers from taking jobs away from the young.

When the boomers are retired, workers and taxpayers will be scarce. Accordingly, we need to scrap such disincentives to work and revamp traditional career patterns to permit and encourage semiretirement, phased retirement, and even unretirement. This is in line with an attack by gerontologists on the simplistic division of life into three boxes—first education, then work, then leisure. Even the American Association of Retired Persons is now fighting for the right of older people to continue working if they want to or need to.

A MARKET-BASED APPROACH TO REDUCING WAGE INEQUALITY

A tragic by-product of the nation's looming fiscal problems is that it has virtually paralyzed us when it comes to thinking creatively about other social issues. As we discussed earlier, for example, the technology revolution and globalization have contributed importantly to widening the gap between high- and low-wage workers. And, if anything, these forces are poised to accelerate. That suggests a worsening outlook for many of the social ills in America that can be traced to the breakdown of the family and a lack of "good" jobs at the low end of the labor market.

Despite the gravity of the problem, the only "remedies" that have any support in Washington are hikes in the minimum wage or protectionist measures to reduce foreign competition. But both remedies could easily do more harm than good. Hikes in the minimum wage are likely to lead to greater unemployment for low-productivity workers. Protectionist measures to ban imports typically lead to retaliation and have been tried before, with disastrous effects. Moreover, the research we have seen suggests that the technology revolution has contributed far more to rising inequality than international competition has. If that is the case, perhaps the rest of the nation should attempt to deal with rising wage inequality by restricting trade with places like Silicon Valley or Redmond, Washington (home of Microsoft).

Economist Edmund Phelps, of Columbia University, proposes a market-based approach to help less-productive workers draw reasonable wages. His proposed solution is a graduated schedule of tax subsidies to firms for every low-wage worker they employ. As firms hire more of these workers, the labor market would tighten and pay levels at the low end of the labor market would rise, narrowing the gap between high- and low-wage workers. Phelps argues persuasively that such a program would be largely self-financing, because its costs would be offset by reductions in the cost of welfare, crime, and medical care—as well as by taxes paid by formerly unemployed workers. But such a program would have initial budget costs of around $110 billion, making it dead on arrival in today's political climate.

Ironically, our current policy paralysis is based on unrealistic promises to tax middle- and upper-class Peters to provide retirement benefits for middle- and upper-class Pauls. As it is, the biggest Social Security checks go to the most affluent households. Even though Social Security was originally set up as a safety net for the truly needy, it has evolved into what Peter Peterson calls "a well-padded hammock for middle- and upper-class retirees."

Moving toward privatized Social Security and Medicare

systems would permit middle- and upper-class citizens to take more responsibility for their retirement savings, while earning better returns in the process. Only by moving in that direction will we have the fiscal latitude to address the social ills that rising wage inequality has generated. Phelps's ideas deserve serious consideration and debate. Tragically, serious debate about how to deal with rising wage inequality has been crowded out of the nation's political agenda, displaced by looming fiscal problems with Social Security and Medicare.

The Big Fix needs to start by fixing Social Security and Medicare. But little progress in addressing the nation's other social ills can be expected if we ignore the problem of rising inequality.

Conclusion

Of Silicon Dreams and
Pyramid Schemes

IN ANCIENT EGYPT, people who thought about the future were dreamers, and their dreams reflected the agrarian society they lived in. Four thousand years later—on the eve of the third millennium—people who think about the future are still dreamers. Their dreams also reflect the society they live in, which is an information-oriented society that has become wealthier than previous generations could possibly have imagined.

Boomernomics, our modern version of Joseph and the pharaoh's story, has been a tale of silicon dreams and pyramid schemes. Our vision of a series of fat years ahead, which we call America's Prime Time, sees the American people continuing to prosper over the next decade as seventy-six million baby boomers move through their peak years of earning, productivity, and perhaps even wisdom. Thanks to a parade of wonders being produced by Silicon Valley and its counterparts around the nation, America remains better-positioned than most countries to benefit from quantum leaps in computing power and telecommunications bandwith that are dramatically increasing the clock speed of the global economy. Likewise, because of its lead in the information sciences, the nation is also poised to widen its lead in biotechnology, which seems likely to become the most important industry of the twenty-first century.

As globalization intensifies and the technology revolution accelerates, inflation should remain low, productivity growth should accelerate, real wages should rise, and long-term interest rates should eventually fall to shockingly low levels of 4 percent or less. Stock market valuations in America's Prime Time could well remain surprisingly high. For the boomer generation, from now through the first ten years of the new millennium, these truly are the good old days.

But good dreams and pleasant reveries are apt to fade. Armed with demographic projections and computer models, we have seen why today's pharaohs can reasonably anticipate that the current period of fat years will be followed by a daunting series of lean years. The lean years can be expected after the baby boomers retire and begin to put massive financial pressure on the Social Security and Medicare pyramid schemes.

Virtually all analysts who have studied the age wave carefully have concluded that our pharaohs need to be doing far more to prepare the nation for the retirement of the baby boomer generation. As we have seen, for example, the Congressional Budget Office recently warned of soaring interest rates and explosive growth of the federal debt during the boomers' retirement years if nothing is done soon to cut the boomers' retirement benefits or to find major new sources of funding. We have also examined the work of other demographically oriented economists who foresee sharp asset price declines—in stocks, bonds, and real estate—during the boomers' retirement years simply due to a potential glut of people who want to sell. Such a financial nightmare, which we call the Big Chill, could be compounded seriously if the government does not soon do more to prepare for the age wave.

For most individuals, preparing for the age wave means saving more, investing in well-diversified and reasonably aggressive portfolios, and not counting on strong double-digit returns in the stock market to persist indefinitely. Even if our scenario for a Japanese-style equity mania during America's Prime Time turns out to be correct, few will be able to get out at the top before the Big Chill arrives. It's better to expect real returns on stocks of 4 to 5 percent in coming years—and to be pleasantly surprised if they are better—than to bet the farm on continuing returns of 15 percent plus.

As a nation, it's time to be honest with ourselves: The Social Security and Medicare pyramid schemes are unsustainable and in need of radical reform. There will be much talk ahead of "strengthening" Social Security and Medicare, but it makes little sense to strengthen programs whose finances resemble illegal Ponzi schemes. "Strengthening" such schemes generally can mean just one thing: cutting net benefits for baby boomers and their children, resulting in even lower returns on their "contributions" to the system. The current Social Security system is approaching its sixty-fifth birthday and should be retired, with dignity, as soon as possible.

As we have seen, an enormous body of research shows that many baby boomers—and most governments around the world—are woefully unprepared for the financial burdens of the age wave. The time to act is now, with more than twenty years to go before the average baby boomer retires.

Real dreamers can hope that the technology revolution

delivers enough miracles to forestall financial crises and generational warfare. Perhaps in twenty years highly automated factories will be spewing forth tens of millions of Star Wars–type intelligent robots every year, or hydrogen-powered cars that get 200 miles per gallon of fuel. If that is the case, then a productivity and wealth revolution fueled by silicon chips and fiber optics could finesse the need for serious preparation for the boomers' retirement years.

We ourselves are technology optimists and would be delighted if such dreams materialize. We would also be delighted to win the lottery. But it would be imprudent—and even dangerous—for baby boomers and their political leaders to depend on divine intervention to provide for the boomers' retirement needs.

The good news is that there is nothing inevitable about our bleak scenario for the boomers' old age. As we have discussed, there are plenty of creative ideas for how America can cope with the age wave, provided we and our leaders get serious posthaste. These include privatizing Social Security, increasing the portability of private pensions and medical insurance, and rethinking the concept of retirement itself.

There are also a number of things you can do to prepare for the age wave. Most important, if your own retirement plan is based on winning the lottery, we encourage you to seek out good financial advice and start a disciplined saving program *now*. It's never too early to start, and for most baby boomers it's still not too late.

If you are concerned about the fat years–lean years scenario, we urge you to contact your local pharoah. Ask what he or she is doing to prepare us for the economic impact of the age wave. Now is the time to vote out of office politicians who refuse to honestly account for and adequately prepare for the coming demographic challenge.

If you have five minutes to spare and have access to the Internet, try out the Cato Institute's Social Security calculator (www.socialsecurity.org) and see how much better you or your children could fare under a privatized system. You are likely to be startled by the results.

Then take a few more moments to send E-mail messages to your congressman and senators. Share the results of your calculations with them and ask if they support moving toward a fully funded, privatized system that will provide better returns. For good measure, ask them to provide you with an estimate of how much your children and grandchildren are expected to pay in taxes when the age wave hits. With millions now connected to the Internet, it has never been easier for people to educate themselves on these issues or to communicate with their lawmakers.

President Clinton has surprised many observers by opening the door to a genuine debate on the future of Social Security and Medicare. In doing so, he has set in motion forces that could lead to fully funded, financially secure, private systems—not only in the United States, but in other major nations as well.

Regardless of whether you agree with our views, now is the time to make your opinion known. The future of your money—and your country—depends on it.

Appendix 1:
Selected References on
Financial Planning

Orman, Suze. *The 9 Steps to Financial Freedom*. New York: Crown, 1997.

    This book is a good place to start if you feel intimidated by money and finance.

Chilton, David. *The Wealthy Barber: Everyone's Commonsense Guide to Becoming Financially Independent*. Rocklin, CA: Prima, 1998.

    This is another easy-to-read book about the basics of personal finance.

Lynch, Peter, and John Rothchild. *Learn to Earn: A Beginner's Guide to the Basics of Investing and Business*. New York: Simon & Schuster, 1995.

    This is another introduction to investing, with tips from a legendary mutual fund manager.

Tobias, Andrew. *The Only Investment Guide You'll Ever Need*. New York: Harcourt Brace, 1996.

    This book is a witty and entertaining classic on personal finance, revised and updated for the 1990s.

Bogle, John C. *Bogle on Mutual Funds: New Perspectives for the Intelligent Investor.* New York: Dell, 1994.

> Warren Buffett called this book "the definitive book on mutual funds."

Malkiel, Burton. *A Random Walk Down Wall Street: Including a Life-Cycle Guide to Personal Investing.* 6th ed. New York: Norton, 1996.

> This book mixes practical advice for individual investors with a sophisticated overview of modern financial theory.

Appendix 2:
Glossary of Terms

dividend yield: This ratio is calculated by dividing a company's annual dividend payments on a per-share basis by its share price. The dividend yield is another common yardstick used by investors to gauge the attractiveness of stocks.

Dow Jones Industries Index: A popular measure of the stock market that is based on an average value of thirty large U.S. stocks.

401(k): A popular retirement savings plan that allows individuals to contribute a percentage of their salary to a savings plan on a tax-free basis. Savings accumulate free of taxes during a worker's career and are only taxed when withdrawn from the plan after retirement. Individuals who withdraw savings from their 401(k) before retirement are subject to a hefty tax on the amount withdrawn.

generational accounting: Most budget accounting focuses on current revenues and expenses of the government. This gives a good picture of where we have been but not where we are going. Politicians frequently attempt to make budgetary policies more palatable by pushing the tax burden off on future generations. Generational accounting prevents such gimmicks. This method of accounting is a comprehensive gauge of all current and future government budgetary policies. As such, it gives a more realistic assessment of the burden of government tax and spending policies on all generations.

gross domestic product (GDP): The total value of goods and services produced in the United States.

gross national product (GNP): The total value of goods and services produced in the United States, plus the amount of profits earned abroad by U.S. companies, less the amount of profits earned by foreign companies operating in the United States. As overall measures of the size of the U.S. economy, GDP and GNP are rough equivalents and are used interchangeably.

individual retirement account (IRA): A popular account that allows individuals to save in a tax-friendly manner. There are three basic kinds of IRAs: traditional, spousal, and Roth. Each IRA has specific restrictions on who may invest, depending on tax status and income level.

medical savings account (MSA): Medical savings accounts would help eliminate the perverse incentives in the current U.S. health care system by allowing individuals to make tax-free deposits each year into their personal MSAs. Funds in the accounts would grow tax-free, and withdrawals would be permitted only for legitimate medical expenses. According to the Health Care Financing Administration, 95 percent of the money Americans now spend in hospitals is someone else's money at the time they spend it. Four fifths of all physicians' payments are now made with other people's money, as are more than three quarters of all medical payments for all purposes. Is it any wonder why health care costs are as high as they are today?

mutual fund: A popular way for investors to get exposure to a wide range of financial assets such as stocks, bonds, real estate, and precious metals. There are many types of mutual funds, and the goals of each type of fund are different. Open-end mutual funds, one of the most popular forms of fund, generally set no limit as to how much money can be invested in the fund. Closed-end funds, on the other hand, limit the amount of money that can be invested in the fund by determining from the fund's inception the number of shares that can be sold to the public.

personal security account (PSA): An account similar to an IRA or 401(k) that would allow workers to put a portion of their payroll tax in their retirement nest eggs. Currently, many young workers are paying money into the Social Security system via a payroll tax that they will never see. The PSA is an innovative and attractive proposal that would allow workers to save for retirement in a tax-friendly manner. PSAs would be subject to some restrictions, but they would be under the sole direction of the workers who owned them.

price-earnings (PE) ratio: This ratio is calculated by dividing a company's stock price on a per-share basis by its earnings per share. For example, if a stock is selling for $10 per share and the company is generating $1 of earnings per share, the PE ratio would be 10 ($10 divided by $1). The PE ratio is a common yardstick used by investors to gauge the attractiveness of stocks. Historically, the stock market, as measured by the S&P 500 stock index, has had an average PE ratio of 15.5.

reversion to the mean: A statistical concept that implies a return to normal or average (which is another word for mean) values. For example, if the stock market is currently trading at a PE ratio of 25 and the long-term average PE ratio is 15.5, investors might expect the market to adjust to the lower long-term average value of 15.5 by "reverting to the mean."

Social Security and Medicare Trust Funds: The former chief actuary of the Social Security Administration, A. Haeworth Robertson, has described these funds as follows: "We are being told that Social Security is accumulating huge trust funds that will help pay retirement benefits to the baby boomers. However, the trust funds are stark naked; there is nothing in them that can be used to pay future benefits. There are only treasury bonds, which are merely promises that the government will collect additional general revenue from the public in the future." Among experts, the joke about the Social Security Trust Fund is that "there's no trust, and no fund."

Standard & Poor's 500 Stock Index (S&P 500): A broad measure of the value of stocks in the United States. The index is an average value of the largest five hundred stocks listed on various U.S. stock exchanges.

Bibliography

Aging in OECD Countries: A Critical Policy Challenge. Social Policy Studies no. 20, Organization for Economic Cooperation and Development, 1997.

Aliber, Robert Z. *Your Time and Your Money: A Lifetime Approach to Money Management.* New York: Basic Books, 1982.

Auerbach, Alan J. *Fiscal Policy: Lessons from Economic Research.* Cambridge: MIT Press, 1997.

Auerbach, Alan J., and Laurence J. Kotlikoff. *The United States' Fiscal and Saving Crises and Their Implications for the Baby Boom Generation.* Report to Merrill Lynch & Co., February 1994.

Bailey, James. *After Thought: The Computer Challenge to Human Intelligence.* New York: BasicBooks, 1996.

Bernheim, Douglas. *The Coming Entitlements Crisis: A Case for Divine Intervention.* Strategic Economic Decisions, Inc., August 1994.

————. *Is the Baby Boom Generation Preparing Adequately for Retirement?* Report for Merrill Lynch, New York, 1993.

Bernstein, Peter L. *Capital Ideas: The Improbable Origins of Modern Wall Street.* New York: Free Press, 1992.

Bogle, John C. *Bogle on Mutual Funds: New Perspectives for the Intelligent Investor.* New York: Dell, 1994.

Brock, H. Woody. *How the Nation That Fired the Most, Hired the Most.* Strategic Economic Decisions Inc., 1996.

Butler, Patrick, and Ted Hall. *A Revolution in Interaction.* The McKinsey Quarterly, 1997, no. 1, McKinsey & Company.

Cairncross, Frances. *The Death of Distance: How the Communications Revolution Will Change Our Lives.* Boston: Harvard Business School Press, 1997.

Chand, Sheetal K., and Albert Jaeger. *Aging Populations and Public Pension Schemes.* International Monetary Fund, Washington, DC, December 1996.

Cochrane, John H. "Where Is the Market Going? Uncertain Facts and Novel Theories." *Federal Reserve Bank of Chicago Economic Perspectives,* November/December 1997.

The Competitive Edge 1998. Morgan Stanley Dean Witter Equity Research, New York.

Cork, David, with Susan Lightstone. *The Pig and the Python: How to Prosper from the Aging Baby Boom.* Rocklin, CA: Prima, 1998.

Cox, W. Michael, and Richard Alm. *The Economy at Light Speed: Technology and Growth in the Information Age—and Beyond.* Federal Reserve Bank of Dallas, 1996 Annual Report.

Cutler, David M., and Louise M. Sheiner. *Policy Options for Long-Term Care.* Chicago: National Bureau of Economic

Research, Studies in the Economics of Aging, University of Chicago Press, 1994.

David, Paul A. "The Dynamo and the Computer: An Historical Perspective on the Modern Productivity Paradox." *American Economic Review* 80, no. 2, 1990, pp. 355–361.

Denning, Peter J., and Robert M. Metcalfe. *Beyond Calculation: The Next Fifty Years of Computing.* New York: Springer-Verlag, 1997.

Dychtwald, Ken, and Joe Flower. *Age Wave: How the Most Important Trend of Our Time Will Change Your Future.* New York: Bantam, 1990.

The Emerging Digital Economy. U.S. Department of Commerce, National Technical Information Service, Springfield, VA, 1998.

Feldstein, Martin. *The Missing Piece in Policy Analysis: Social Security Reform.* American Economic Review Papers and Proceedings, May 1996.

Foot, David K., with Daniel Stoffman. *Boom Bust & Echo: How to Profit from the Coming Demographic Shift.* Toronto: Macfarlane Walter & Ross, 1996.

Gates, Bill. *The Road Ahead.* New York: Penguin, 1995.

Gianturco, Michael. *The Market That Beats the Market: How to Profit in Technology Stocks and Funds.* New York: Little, Brown, 1995.

Gilder, George. *Microcosm: The Quantum Revolution in Economics and Technology.* New York: Simon and Schuster, 1989.

———. *Telecosm.* New York: American Heritage Custom Publishing, 1996.

Gokhale, Jagadeesh, Laurence J. Kotlikoff, and John Sabelhaus. "Understanding the Postwar Decline in U.S. Saving: A Cohort Analysis." *Brookings Papers on Economic Activity* 1, 1996, pp. 315–390.

Goodman, John C., and Gerald L. Musgrave. *Patient Power: The Free-Enterprise Alternative to Clinton's Health Plan.* Washington, DC: Cato Institute, 1994.

Grace, Eric S. *Biotechnology Unzipped: Promises and Realities.* Washington, DC: Joseph Henry Press, 1997.

Gross, William H. *Everything You've Heard About Investing Is Wrong!: How to Profit in the Coming Post-Bull Markets.* New York: Times Business, Random House, 1997.

Hagel, John III, and Arthur G. Armstrong. *Net Gain: Expanding Markets Through Virtual Communities.* Boston: Harvard Business School Press, 1997.

Hale, David. *The Economic Consequences of the American Mutual Fund Boom.* Davos World Economic Forum, February 1994.

Haseltine, William: "Discovering Genes for New Medicines." *Scientific American,* March 1997.

Hobbs, Frank B., with Bonnie L. Damon. *65+ in the United States.* Current Population Reports Special Studies, U.S. Department of Commerce, Washington, DC, 1996.

Homer, Sidney. *A History of Interest Rates,* 3d ed. Piscataway, NJ: Rutgers University Press, 1963.

Homer, Sidney, and Richard Johannesen. *The Price of Money 1946–1969.* Piscataway, NJ: Rutgers University Press, 1969.

Jones, Landon Y. *Great Expectations: America and The Baby Boom Generation.* New York: Coward, McCann & Geoghegan, 1980.

Judy, Richard W., and Carol D'Amico. *Workforce 2020: Work*

and *Workers in the 21st Century.* Indianapolis, IN: Hudson Institute, 1997.

Kaku, Michio. *Visions: How Science Will Revolutionize the 21st Century.* New York: Anchor Books, Doubleday, 1997.

Karpel, Craig S. *The Retirement Myth.* New York: Harper-Collins, 1995.

Kelly, Kevin. *Out of Control: The Rise of Neo-Biological Civilization.* Reading, MA: Addison-Wesley, 1994.

Kotlikoff, Laurence J. *Generational Accounting: Knowing Who Pays, and When, for What We Spend.* New York: Free Press, 1992.

Krueger, Alan. *What's Up with Wages?* Goldman Sachs, New York, November 13, 1997.

Krugman, Paul. *The Age of Diminished Expectations: U.S. Economic Policy in the 1990s.* Cambridge: MIT Press, 1990.

Long-Term Budgetary Pressures and Policy Options. Congressional Budget Office, Washington, DC, March 1997.

Mackenzie, G.A., Philip Gerson, and Alfredo Cuevas. *Pension Regimes and Saving.* International Monetary Fund, Washington DC, August 1997.

Mahar, Maggie. "Eden for Sale." *Barron's,* July 3, 1995.

Mandel, Michael J. *The High Risk Society: Peril and Promise in the New Economy.* New York: Times Business, Random House, 1996.

McFadden, Daniel. *Demographics, the Housing Market, and the Welfare of the Elderly.* Chicago: National Bureau of Economic Research, Studies in the Economics of Aging, University of Chicago Press, 1994.

Medoff, James, and Andrew Harless. *The Indebted Society:*

Anatomy of an Ongoing Disaster. New York: Little, Brown, 1996.

Morgan, Donald P. *Will the Shift to Stocks and Bonds by Households Be Destabilizing?* Federal Reserve Bank of Kansas City Economic Review, Second Quarter 1994.

Negroponte, Nicholas. *Being Digital.* New York: Knopf, 1995.

1998 Annual Report of the Board of Trustees of the Federal Old-Age and Survivors Insurance and Disability Insurance Trust Funds. Washington, DC, April 28, 1998.

Passell, Peter. "The Year Is 2010. Do You Know Where Your Bull Is?" *New York Times,* 1996.

Paulus, John D. *Secular Trends in U.S. Stock Prices.* Unpublished manuscript, 1998.

Peterson, Peter G. *Will America Grow Up Before It Grows Old?* New York: Random House, 1996.

Phelps, Edmund. *Rewarding Work: How to Restore Participation and Self-Support to Free Enterprise.* Cambridge: Harvard University Press, 1997.

Piñera, José. *Empowering Workers: The Privatization of Social Security in Chile.* Washington, DC: Cato Institute, 1996.

Posner, Richard A. *Aging and Old Age.* Chicago: University of Chicago Press, 1995.

Reading, Brian. *Japan: The Coming Collapse.* London: Weidenfeld and Nicolson, 1992.

Robertson, A. Haeworth. *The Big Lie: What Every Baby Boomer Should Know About Social Security and Medicare.* Retirement Policy Institute, Washington, DC, 1997.

Rothschild, Michael. *Bionomics: Economy as Ecosystem.* New York: Henry Holt, 1990.

Samuelson, Paul A. "The Judgment of Economic Science on Rational Portfolio Management: Indexing, Timing, and Long-Horizon Effects." *Journal of Portfolio Management* 16, no. 1, 1989.

Schieber, Sylvester J., and John Shoven. *The Consequences of Population Aging on Private Pension Fund Saving and Asset Markets.* Center for Economic Policy Research, Publication no. 363, September 1993.

————. *Public Policy Toward Pensions.* Cambridge: MIT Press, 1997.

Schonfeld, Erick. "Betting on the Boomers." *Fortune,* December 25, 1995.

Shipman, William. *Retiring with Dignity: Social Security vs. Private Markets.* Washington, DC: Cato Institute, August 14, 1995.

Siegel, Jeremy J. *Stocks for the Long Run.* New York: McGraw Hill, 1998.

Silver, Lee M. *Remaking Eden: Cloning and Beyond in a Brave New World.* New York: Avon, 1997.

Simon, Julian L. *The State of Humanity.* Cambridge: Blackwell, 1995.

Sterling, William, and Stephen Waite. *Building Nations: The Case for U.S. Capital Goods.* Merrill Lynch & Co., November 1992.

————. *The Twilight of Inflation.* Merrill Lynch & Co., May 1993.

Steuerle, C. Eugene, and Jon M. Bakija. *Retooling Social Security for the 21st Century: Right and Wrong Approaches to Reform.* Washington, DC: Urban Institute Press, 1994.

Tanner, Michael. *Privatizing Social Security: A Big Boost for the Poor.* Washington, DC: Cato Institute, July 26, 1996.

Tapscott, Don. *Growing Up Digital: The Rise of the Net Generation.* New York: McGraw-Hill, 1998.

Turner, Garth. *2015 After the Boom: How to Prosper Through the Coming Retirement Crisis.* Toronto: Key Porter Books, 1995.

Waldrop, M. Mitchell. *Complexity: The Emerging Science at the Edge of Order and Chaos.* New York: Simon and Schuster, 1992.

Wolfe, John R. *The Coming Health Crisis: Who Will Pay for Care for the Aged in the 21st Century.* Chicago: University of Chicago Press, 1993.

World Economic Outlook. *Globalization: Opportunities and Challenges.* International Monetary Fund, Washington, DC, May 1997.

The World in 2020: Towards a New Global Age. Organization for Economic Cooperation and Development, 1997.

Wriston, Walter. *The Twilight of Sovereignty: How the Information Revolution Is Transforming Our World.* New York: Charles Scribner's Sons, 1992.

Index

ABOUT THE AUTHORS

WILLIAM STERLING is well known on Wall Street as an investment strategist with a unique global perspective. He is currently head of global equities for Credit Suisse Asset Management, leading a group of more than one hundred investment professionals around the world. His staff manages more than $30 billion in equity investments, and as Executive Director he has direct responsibility for more than $5 billion in global and international funds, working for Credit Suisse Asset Management's U.S. affiliate, BEA Associates. After obtaining a Ph.D. in economics from Harvard University, Sterling worked as an economist for Merrill Lynch in Tokyo in the late 1980s, during Japan's financial market boom. From 1989 to 1995 he headed Merrill's international economics group and conducted research on trends in international interest rates, exchange rates, and money flows to emerging markets. Sterling is known for his ability to explain complex and technical subjects in plain English. He is widely sought as a speaker and commentator on global investment trends and has made frequent appearances on CNN, CNBC, and other major international news networks. He lives in New Jersey with his wife and three children.

STEPHEN WAITE has spent the past twelve years working on Wall Street for several of the world's premier financial services firms. He is currently Portfolio Manager and Global Strategist for BEA Associates, an affiliate of Credit Suisse Asset Management in New York. He is part of a group of investment professionals who manage more than $30 billion of equity assets worldwide.

Prior to joining BEA Associates, Steve was Senior European Economist for Merrill Lynch in London, England. He shared responsibility with William Sterling for the firm's international economic and financial market analysis. Previous to Merrill Lynch, Steve was an international economic consultant to The Capital Group, a Los Angeles–based asset management firm. He began his career on Wall Street as an economist for Morgan Stanley & Co. in New York.

Steve has written extensively on global economic and financial market issues. His work has been published in several books and professional journals and has been cited in publications such as *The Wall Street Journal, The Economist,* and *Business Week.* Steve received his master's degree in economics from the Pennsylvania State University and has a bachelor's degree in economics from Central Michigan University. A former semiprofessional musician who still enjoys playing, Steve completed a summer guitar program at the Berklee School of Music in Boston, Massachusetts. He resides in Connecticut with his wife, Lisa, and daughter, Madeleine.

A Note on The Library of Contemporary Thought

This exciting new monthly series tackles today's most provocative, fascinating, and relevant issues, giving top opinion makers a forum to explore topics that matter urgently to themselves and their readers. Some will be think pieces. Some will be research oriented. Some will be journalistic in nature. The form is wide open, but the aim is the same: to say things that need saying.

Now available from
THE LIBRARY OF CONTEMPORARY THOUGHT

VINCENT BUGLIOSI
NO ISLAND OF SANITY
Paula Jones v. Bill Clinton
The Supreme Court on Trial

JOHN FEINSTEIN
THE FIRST COMING
Tiger Woods: Master or Martyr?

PETE HAMILL
NEWS IS A VERB
Journalism at the End of the
Twentieth Century

CARL HIAASEN
TEAM RODENT
How Disney Devours the World

SEYMOUR M. HERSH
AGAINST ALL ENEMIES
Gulf War Syndrome: The War
Between America's Ailing
Veterans and Their Government

EDWIN SCHLOSSBERG
INTERACTIVE EXCELLENCE
Defining and Developing New
Standards for the Twenty-first
Century

ANNA QUINDLEN
HOW READING CHANGED
MY LIFE

Coming from
THE LIBRARY OF CONTEMPORARY THOUGHT

*America's most original writers
give you a piece of their minds*

Jimmy Carter
Susan Isaacs
Stephen Jay Gould
Nora Ephron
Jonathan Kellerman
Robert Hughes
Joe Klein
Donna Tartt
Walter Moseley
Don Imus

**Look for these titles coming soon from
The Library of Contemporary Thought**

JIMMY CARTER
THE VIRTUES OF AGING

SUSAN ISAACS
BRAVE DAMES AND WIMPETTES
What Women Are Really
Doing on Screen and Page